SECOND EDITION

TOP NOTCH

English for Today's World

FUNDAMENTALS

A

WITH WORKBOOK

Joan Saslow • Allen Ascher

With *Top Notch Pop Songs and Karaoke*
by Rob Morsberger

سرشناسه:	سسلو، جون ام. Saslow, Joan M
عنوان و نام پدیدآور:	Top Notch: English for Today's World: Fundamentals A/ Joan Saslow, Allen Ascher
مشخصات نشر:	تهران: کتابدوستان، ۱۳۹۱ = ۲۰۱۲م.
مشخصات ظاهری:	۱۴۴ ص.: مصور (رنگی)؛ ۲۲ × ۲۹ س.م.
وضعیت فهرست‌نویسی:	فیپا.
یادداشت:	انگلیسی.
یادداشت:	افست از روی ویراست دوم ۲۰۱۱م. نیویورک.
آوانویسی عنوان:	تاپ ناچ...
موضوع:	زبان انگلیسی -- کتاب‌های درسی برای خارجیان
شناسه افزوده:	آشر، آلن
شناسه افزوده:	Ascher, Allen
رده‌بندی کنگره:	۱۳۹۱ ۲۱۷ت۵ص/PE۱۱۲۸
رده‌بندی دیویی:	۴۲۸/۲۴
شماره کتابشناسی ملی:	۲۸۱۷۹۸۳

Top Notch English for Today's World Fundamental A with Workbook، مؤلفین: Joan Saslow & Allen Ascher، چاپ: چاپخانه نمرهقام، چاپ اول: ۱۳۹۲، تیراژ: ۳۰۰۰ نسخه، ناشر: انتشارات کتابدوستان، مرکز پخش: انتشارات رهنما، آدرس: مقابل دانشگاه تهران، خیابان فروردین، نبش خیابان شهدای ژاندارمری، پلاک ۱۱۲، تلفن: ۶۶۴۰۰۹۲۷، ۶۶۴۱۶۶۰۴، ۶۶۴۸۱۶۶۲، فاکس: ۶۶۴۶۷۴۲۴، فروشگاه رهنما، سعادت‌آباد، خیابان علامه طباطبایی جنوبی، بین ۴۰ و ۴۲ شرقی، پلاک ۲۹، تلفن: ۸۸۶۹۴۱۰۲، آدرس فروشگاه شماره ۴: خیابان پیروزی نبش خیابان سوم نیروی هوایی، تلفن: ۷۷۴۸۲۵۰۵، نمایشگاه کتاب رهنما مقابل دانشگاه تهران پاساژ فروزنده، تلفن: ۶۶۹۵۰۹۵۷

قیمت: ۱۵۰۰۰۰ ریال

Top Notch: English for Today's World   Fundamentals A with Workbook, Second Edition

Copyright © 2011 by Pearson Education, Inc.
All rights reserved. No part of this publication may be reproduced, stored in a retrieval system, or transmitted in any form or by any means, electronic, mechanical, photocopying, recording, or otherwise, without the prior permission of the publisher.

Pearson Education, 10 Bank Street, White Plains, NY 10606

Staff credits: The people who made up the *Top Notch Fundamentals* team—representing editorial, design, production, and manufacturing—are Rhea Banker, Elizabeth Carlson, Aerin Csigay, Mindy DePalma, Dave Dickey, Warren Fischbach, Aliza Greenblatt, Ray Keating, Mike Kemper, Maria Pia Marrella, Jessica Miller-Smith, Barbara Sabella, Martin Yu, and Wendy Wolf.

Cover design: Rhea Banker
Cover photo: Sprint/Corbis
Text design: Elizabeth Carlson and Wendy Wolf
Text composition: Quarasan!
Text font: 9/10 Stone Sans, ITC Stone Sans

Library of Congress Cataloging-in-Publication Data

Saslow, Joan M.
  Top notch : English for today's world / Joan Saslow, Allen Ascher ; with Top Notch pop songs and Karaoke by
    Rob Morsberger. — 2nd ed.
      p. cm.
  ISBN 0-13-246988-X (set) — ISBN 0-13-247038-1 (v. 1) — ISBN 0-13-247048-9 (v. 2) — ISBN 0-13-247027-6
  (v. 3) 1. English language — Textbooks for foreign speakers. 2. English language — Problems, exercises, etc.
  I. Ascher, Allen. II. Title.
PE1128.S2757 2011
428.2'4 — dc22
                    2010019162

ISBN 10: 0-13-246989-8
ISBN 13: 978-0-13-246989-0

Photo credits: All original photography by Sharon Hoogstraten and David Mager. Page 4 (1) Jose Luis PelaezInc./Corbis, (2) Dex Images/Corbis, (3) Royalty-Free/Corbis, (4) Mark Richards/PhotoEdit, Inc., (5) Jim Arbogast/Getty Images, (6) Getty Images, (7) James P. Blair/Corbis, (8) Spencer Grant/PhotoEdit, Inc., (9) Kevin Winter/Getty Images, (10) Reuters NewMedia Inc./Corbis; p. 5 (left) AP Images/Chris Polk, (middle left) Alexander Tamargo/Getty Images, (middle right) Courtesy of Korean Concert Society, (right) AP Images/Petr David Josek; p. 6 (1) Alan Bolesta/Index Stock Imagery, (2) Kim Steele/Getty Images, (3) Tom McCarthy/PhotoEdit, Inc., (4) Thinkstock, (5) Jose Luis Pelaez Inc./Corbis, (6) Getty Images, (7) Getty Images, (8) Getty Images, p. 8 (top) Shutterstock.com; p. 10 (left) Robert Mora/Getty Images, (middle left) Kabik/Retna Ltd./Corbis, (middle right) Reuters NewMedia Inc./Corbis, (right) Piero Pomponi/Liaison/Getty Images; p. 13 (top) Shutterstock.com; (1) Shutterstock.com, (2) Shutterstock.com, (3) Shutterstock.com, p. 16 (left) Shutterstock.com; p. 18 (Gehry) Thierry Prat/Sygma/Corbis, (de Lucia) Alonso Gonzales/Reuters/Corbis, (Sharapova) Reuters/Corbis, (Travolta) AP Images/Rob Griffith, (Kidjo) Michael Latz AFP/Getty Images, (Yoshimoto) Tiziana Fabi/AFP/Getty Images; p. 19 (background) iStockphoto.com; p. 20 (1) Bill Aron/PhotoEdit, Inc., (2) Getty Images, (3) Steven Dunwell/Getty Images, (4) Shutterstock.com, (5) Jeff Greenberg/PhotoEdit, Inc., (6) Dave Bartruff/Corbis; p. 22 (1) Shutterstock.com, (2) Shutterstock.com, (3) NRT-Travel/Alamy, (4) Shutterstock.com, (5) Shutterstock.com; p. 24 (1) Shutterstock.com, (2) Shutterstock.com, (3) Shutterstock.com, (4) Shutterstock.com, (5) Shutterstock.com; p. 26 (Lee) Shutterstock.com, (Beck) Shutterstock.com, (White) Shutterstock.com; p. 28 (background) Shutterstock.com, (1 left) Shutterstock.com, (1 right) Shutterstock.com, (2 left) Shutterstock.com, (2 right) Shutterstock.com, (3 left) Shutterstock.com, (3 right) Shutterstock.com, (4 left) Shutterstock.com, (4 right) Shutterstock.com, (5 left) Shutterstock.com, (5 right) Shutterstock.com, (6 left) Shutterstock.com, (6 right) Shutterstock.com; p. 29 Shutterstock.com; p. 30 (1) Douglas Kirkland/Corbis, (2) Lisa O'Connor/ZUMA/Corbis, (4) Melissa Gunn, (7&8) Shutterstock.com, (bottom 2) Arturo Piñango, (bottom 3) Shutterstock.com; p. 31 (1) Antony Nagelmann/Getty Images; p. 32 (top) Shutterstock.com, (bottom) images/iStockphoto.com; p. 33 (top) Picture Partners/Alamy; p. 34 (left) Reuters NewMedia Inc./Corbis, (middle) Angela Weiss/Getty Images, (right) Vera Anderson/Getty Images; p. 35 (top) David Lok/SuperStock, (bottom) Darama/Corbis; p. 38 (1) Alamy, (2) Rick Gomez/Corbis, (3) AFP/Corbis, (4) Douglas Kirkland/Corbis, (5 inset) Original Films/The Kobal Collection, (5) Graham French/Masterfile, (6) Stephane Cardinale/People Avenue/Corbis; p. 39 (dance) Chuck Savage/Corbis, (movie) Fox Searchlight/Photofest, (concert) Shutterstock.com; p. 41 (top) Stephanie Maze/Corbis; p. 42 (1-4) Gilbert Duclos; p. 43 (left) EyeWire Collection/Getty Images, (middle) Shutterstock.com, (right) Solus-Veer/Corbis; p. 44 (1) Shutterstock.com, (2) Dorling Kindersley, (3) iStockphoto.com, (4) Jonathan Kantor/Getty Images, (5) FashionSyndicatePress.com, (6) Shutterstock.com, (7) Ryan McVay/Getty Images, (8 left) (5) FashionSyndicatePress.com, (8 right) Shutterstock.com, (9) Getty Images; p. 46 (left) Getty Images; p. 47 (left background) Shutterstock.com, (right background) Shutterstock.com, (pants) David Young-Wolff/PhotoEdit, Inc., (tie) Shutterstock.com, (suit) Dorling Kindersley, (sweater) Shutterstock.com, (two-piece) Dorling Kindersley, (shoes) Michael Newman/PhotoEdit, Inc.; p. 48 (1) Shutterstock.com, (2) Shutterstock.com, (4) iStockphoto.com, (7) Shutterstock.com, (8) Shutterstock.com, (9) Comstock Images/Getty Images, (10) Shutterstock.com; p. 49 Jupiterimages/BananaStock/Alamy; p. 50 (red shoes) Shutterstock.com, (purple shoes) Shutterstock.com, (brown shoes) Shutterstock.com; p. 58 (top) Courtesy iRobot Corporation, (middle) Courtesy iRobot Corporation, (left) Reuters/Toshiyuki Aizawa, (bottom) Zucchetti Centro Sistemi spa, (bottom background) Shutterstock.com; p. 59 (top background) Shutterstock.com, (bottom background) Shutterstock.com, (bottom) Shutterstock.com; p. 63 (middle) Chuck Savage/Corbis; p. 126 (2) Picture Quest/Jim Pickerell/Stock Connection, (3) Keith Brofsky/Getty Images, (4) Arthur S. Aubry/Getty Images, (5) Royalty-Free/Corbis, (6) Shutterstock.com, (9) Kwame Kikomo/Superstock, (10) Royalty-Free/Corbis, (12) Jonathan Nouvok/The Image Works, (16) Comstock Images, (17) Getty Images, (18) Royalty-Free/Corbis; p. 127 (top left to right) Corbis, Doug Pensinger/Getty Images, Royalty-Free/Corbis, John Henley/Corbis, iStockphoto.com, (4) Vittoriano Rastelli/Corbis, (5) Corbis, (6) Corbis, (7) Corbis, (8) Tom & Dee Ann McCarthy/Corbis, (9) Tom Wagner/Corbis Saba, (10) Jeff Greenberg/PhotoEdit, Inc., (11) Getty Images, (12) Michael Newman/PhotoEdit, Inc., (13) Bill Bachmann/PhotoEdit, Inc., (14) Tom Carter/PhotoEdit, Inc., (15) Jeff Greenberg/PhotoEdit, Inc., p. 128 (top 1) Dorling Kindersley, (top 2) Duane Rieder, (top 3) Dorling Kindersley, (1) Dorling Kindersley, (2) Corbis, (3) Dorling Kindersley, (5) Kazuhiro Nogi/AFP/Getty Images, (7) Robbie Jack Photography, (8) Getty Images; p. 129 (3) Dorling Kindersley, (4) Comstock, (bottom 1) Robert Brenner/PhotoEdit, Inc., p. W1 (1) Cat Gwynn/Getty Images, (2) Shutterstock.com, (3) Shutterstock.com, (4) Shutterstock.com; p. W2 (top) Courtesy of Korean Concert Society, (bottom) AP Images/Petr David Josek; p. W4 (left) Steve Finn/Getty Images, (right) Frank Micelotta/Getty Images; p. W5 (left) Shutterstock.com, (middle left) Mark Richards/PhotoEdit Inc., (middle right) Shutterstock.com, (right) Shutterstock.com; p. W13 (top) Shutterstock.com, (bottom) Jeff Greenberg/PhotoEdit Inc.; p. W15 (top) Shutterstock.com, (middle top) Shutterstock.com, (middle bottom) Jeff Greenberg/PhotoEdit Inc., (bottom) Shutterstock.com; p. W18 (1) Tim Graham/Corbis, (2) Corbis, (3) Shutterstock.com, (4) Tim Graham/Corbis, (5) Tim Graham/Corbis; p. W43 (top) Reuters/Corbis, (bottom left) Bettmann/Corbis, (bottom right) Miramax/Dimension Films/The Kobal Collection; p. W44 (1) Picture Quest/Jim Pickerell/Stock Connection, (2) Keith Brofsky/Getty Images, (3) Royalty-Free/Corbis, (4) Shutterstock.com, (5) Shutterstock.com, (6) Shutterstock.com; p. W45 (top middle) Shutterstock.com, (top right) Shutterstock.com, (bottom left) Shutterstock.com, (bottom middle) Tom & Dee Ann McCarthy/Corbis, (bottom right) Corbis; p. W46 (1) Shutterstock.com; p. W47 (3) Shutterstock.com, (4) Shutterstock.com, (5) Shutterstock.com, (middle left) Robert Brenner/PhotoEdit, Inc., (middle right) Shutterstock.com, (bottom middle) Shutterstock.com.

Illustration credits: Steve Attoe, pp. W2, W26 (bottom); Kenneth Batelman, pp. 37 (bottom center), 48 (top), 61, W15; John Ceballos, pp. 43, 51 (top); Pascal Dejong, p. 11; Bob Doucet, p. 27; Ingo Fast, p. 21 (top); Leanne Franson, pp. W3, W7, W19, W20, W23, W40 (top); Scott Fray, p. 53; Brian Hughes, pp. 22, 25 (bottom), 36 (top), 46; Steve Hutchings, p. W37; Robert Kemp, p. 20; Jim Kopp, p. 24; Pat Lewis, p. 57 (right); Suzanne Morgensen, pp. 45 (bottom), W21, W24; Andy Myer, pp. 7, 17; Sandy Nichols, pp. 10, 37 (top); NSV Productions, p. 37 (bottom left, bottom right); Dusan Petricic, pp. 44, 45 (top), 60 (bottom), W1, W26 (top), W31 (top), W34, W46; Michelle Rabagliati, pp.W29, W31 (bottom); Phil Scheuer, pp. 2, 25 (top), 54, 56, 57, W40 (bottom); Steve Schulman, pp. W30, W32; Steven Stankiewicz, p. 21 (bottom); Don Stewart, p. 48 (center, bottom); Neil Stewart, pp. 36 (center right), W13, W14 (bottom), W15 (right), W17, W27 (top), W36; Meryl Treatner, p. 37 (center); Anna Veltfort, pp. 12, 52, W8; Patrick Welsh, pp. W14 (top), W25 (top right, top left); XNR Productions, pp. 36 (bottom), 60 (top).

Printed in the United States of America
1 2 3 4 5 6 7 8 9 10 – V042 – 15 14 13 12 11

CONTENTS

Learning Objectives for Fundamentals A and Fundamentals B iv
To the Teacher viii
About Your *ActiveBook* Self-Study Disc ix

Welcome to Top Notch! 1
UNIT 1 Names and Occupations 4
UNIT 2 About People 12
UNIT 3 Places and How to Get There 20
UNIT 4 Family 28
UNIT 5 Events and Times 36
UNIT 6 Clothes 44
UNIT 7 Activities 52
Units 1-7 Review 60

REFERENCE CHARTS

Countries and nationalities 125
Numbers 100 to 1,000,000,000 125
Irregular verbs 125
Pronunciation table 125

Vocabulary Booster 126
Grammar Booster 136
Top Notch Pop Lyrics 147

WORKBOOK

UNIT 1 . . . . W1
UNIT 2 . . . . W7
UNIT 3 . . . . W13
UNIT 4 . . . . W18
UNIT 5 . . . . W23
UNIT 6 . . . . W29
UNIT 7 . . . . W36
Units 1-7 Review W42
About the Authors . . . . last page

Learning Objectives

Top Notch Fundamentals is designed for true beginning students or for students needing the support of a very low-level beginning course. No prior knowledge of English is assumed or necessary.

Unit	Communication Goals	Vocabulary	Grammar

1 **Names and Occupations** page 4	• Tell a classmate your occupation
	• Identify your classmates
	• Spell names
		• Occupations
		• The alphabet
		VOCABULARY BOOSTER
		• More occupations
			• Verb be:
			  ◦ Singular and plural statements, contractions
			  ◦ Yes / no questions and short answers
			  ◦ Common errors
			• Subject pronouns
			• Articles a / an
			• Nouns:
			  ◦ Singular and plural / Common and proper
			GRAMMAR BOOSTER • Extra practice

2 **About People** page 12	• Introduce people • Tell someone your first and last name • Get someone's contact information	• Relationships (non-family) • Titles • First and last names • Numbers 0–20 **VOCABULARY BOOSTER** • More relationships	• Possessive nouns and adjectives • Be from / Questions with Where, common errors • Verb be: information questions with What **GRAMMAR BOOSTER** • Extra practice
3 **Places and How to Get There** page 20	• Talk about locations • Discuss how to get places • Discuss transportation	• Places in the neighborhood • Locations • Ways to get places • Means of transportation • Destinations **VOCABULARY BOOSTER** • More places	• Verb be: questions with Where • Subject pronoun it • The imperative • By to express means of transportation **GRAMMAR BOOSTER** • Extra practice

4 **Family** page 28	• Identify people in your family
	• Describe your relatives
	• Talk about your family
		• Family relationships
		• Adjectives to describe people
		• Numbers 21–101
		VOCABULARY BOOSTER
		• More adjectives
			• Verb be:
			  ◦ Questions with Who and common errors
			  ◦ With adjectives
			  ◦ Questions with How old
			• Adverbs very and so
			• Verb have / has: affirmative statements
			GRAMMAR BOOSTER • Extra practice

5 **Events and Times** page 36	• Confirm that you're on time • Talk about the time of an event • Ask about birthdays	• What time is it? • Early, on time, late • Events • Days of the week • Ordinal numbers • Months of the year **VOCABULARY BOOSTER** • More events	• Verb be: questions about time • Prepositions in, on, and at for dates and times • Common errors **GRAMMAR BOOSTER** • Extra practice

6 **Clothes** page 44	• Give and accept a compliment
	• Ask for colors and sizes
	• Describe clothes
		• Clothes
		• Colors and sizes
		• Opposite adjectives to describe clothes
		VOCABULARY BOOSTER
		• More clothes
			• Demonstratives this, that, these, those
			• The simple present tense: like, want, need, and have:
			  ◦ Affirmative and negative statements
			  ◦ Questions and short answers
			  ◦ Spelling rules and contractions
			  ◦ Adjective placement and common errors
			• One and ones
			GRAMMAR BOOSTER • Extra practice

7 **Activities** page 52
Units 1-7 Review page 60
	• Talk about morning and evening activities
	• Describe what you do in your free time
	• Discuss household chores
		• Daily activities at home
		• Leisure activities
		• Household chores
		VOCABULARY BOOSTER
		• More household chores
			• The simple present tense:
			  ◦ Third-person singular spelling rules
			  ◦ Questions with When and What time
			  ◦ Questions with How often, time expressions
			  ◦ Questions with Who as subject, common errors
			• Frequency adverbs and time expressions:
			  ◦ Usage, placement, and common errors
			GRAMMAR BOOSTER • Extra practice

Conversation Strategies	Listening / Pronunciation	Reading / Writing
• Use <u>And you?</u> to show interest in another person • Use <u>Excuse me</u> to initiate a conversation • Use <u>Excuse me?</u> to indicate you haven't heard or didn't understand • Use <u>Thanks!</u> to acknowledge someone's complying with a request	**Listening task:** • Circle the letter you hear • Identify correct spelling of names • Write the name you hear spelled • Identify the correct occupation • Write the missing information: names and occupations **Pronunciation:** • Syllables	**Reading Text:** • Simple forms and business cards **Writing Task:** • Write affirmative and negative statements about people in a picture
• Identify someone's relationship to you when making an introduction • Use <u>too</u> to reciprocate a greeting • Begin a question with <u>And</u> to indicate you want additional information • Repeat part of a question to clarify • Repeat information to confirm	**Listening task:** • Complete statements about relationships • Circle the correct information • Fill in names, phone numbers, and e-mail addresses you hear **Pronunciation:** • Stress in two-word pairs	**Reading Text:** • Short descriptions of famous people, their occupations, and countries of origin **Writing Task:** • Write sentences about your relationships
• Use <u>You're welcome</u> to formally acknowledge thanks • Use <u>OK</u> to acknowledge advice • Use <u>What about you?</u> to show interest in another person	**Listening task:** • Write the places you hear • Write the directions you hear, using affirmative and negative imperatives • Circle the means of transportation • Write <u>by</u> phrases, check destinations you hear **Pronunciation:** • Falling intonation for questions with <u>Where</u>	**Reading Texts:** • Simple maps and diagrams • Introductions of people, their relationships and occupations, where they live, and how they get to work **Writing Task:** • Write questions and answers about the places in a complex picture
• Use <u>Well,...</u> to indicate one is deciding how to begin a response • Use <u>And how about...?</u> to ask for more information • Use <u>Really?</u> to show interest or mild surprise	**Listening task:** • Identify the picture of a relative being described • Choose the adjective that describes the people mentioned in a conversation **Pronunciation:** • Number contrasts	**Reading Texts:** • A family tree • A magazine article about famous actors and their families **Writing Task:** • Write a description of the people in your family
• Use <u>Uh-oh</u> to indicate you may have made a mistake • Use <u>Look</u> to focus someone's attention on something • Use <u>Great!</u> to show enthusiasm for an idea • Offer someone best wishes on his or her birthday	**Listening task:** • Identify events and circle the correct times • Write the events you hear in a date book • Circle the dates you hear **Pronunciation:** • Sentence rhythm	**Reading Texts:** • A world map with time zones • Events posters • Conversations • A zodiac calendar **Writing Task:** • Write about events at your school or in your city
• Acknowledge a compliment with <u>Thank you</u> • Apologize with <u>I'm sorry</u> when expressing disappointing information • Use <u>That's too bad</u> to express disappointment • Use <u>What about you?</u> to ask for someone's opinion • Use <u>Well</u> to soften a strong opinion	**Listening task:** • Confirm details about clothes • Determine colors of garments **Pronunciation:** • Plural endings	**Reading Text:** • A sales flyer from a department store **Writing Task:** • Write sentences about the clothes you have, need, want, and like
• Say <u>Me?</u> to give yourself time to think of a personal response • Use <u>Well</u> to introduce a lengthy response • Use <u>So</u> to introduce a conversation topic • Use <u>How about you?</u> to ask for parallel information • Say <u>Sure</u> to indicate a willingness to answer • Begin a response to an unexpected question with <u>Oh</u>	**Listening task:** • Match chores to the people who performed them **Pronunciation:** • Third-person singular verb endings	**Reading Text:** • A review of housekeeping robots **Writing Tasks:** • Write five sentences about robots • Describe your typical week, using adverbs of frequency and time expressions

Unit	Communication Goals	Vocabulary	Grammar

8 **Home and Neighborhood** page 64	• Describe your neighborhood
	• Ask about someone's home
	• Talk about furniture and appliances
		• Types of buildings
		• Places in the neighborhood
		• Rooms
		• Furniture and appliances
		VOCABULARY BOOSTER
		• More home and office vocabulary
			• The simple present tense:
			  ◦ Questions with <u>Where</u>, prepositions of place
			• <u>There is</u> and <u>there are</u>:
			  ◦ Statements and <u>yes</u> / <u>no</u> questions
			  ◦ Contractions and common errors
			• Questions with <u>How many</u>
			GRAMMAR BOOSTER • Extra practice

9 **Activities and Plans** page 72	• Describe today's weather
	• Ask about people's activities
	• Discuss plans
		• Weather expressions
		• Present and future time expressions
		VOCABULARY BOOSTER
		• More weather vocabulary
			• The present continuous:
			  ◦ Statements: form and usage
			  ◦ <u>Yes</u> / <u>no</u> questions
			  ◦ Information questions
			  ◦ For future plans
			• The present participle: spelling rules
			GRAMMAR BOOSTER • Extra practice

10 **Food** page 80	• Discuss ingredients for a recipe • Offer and ask for foods • Invite someone to join you at the table	• Foods and drinks • Places to keep food in a kitchen • Containers and quantities • Cooking verbs **VOCABULARY BOOSTER** • More vegetables and fruits	• Count nouns and non-count nouns: ◦ Meaning, form, and common errors • Count nouns: <u>How many</u> / <u>Are there any</u> • Non-count nouns: <u>How much</u> / <u>Is there any</u> • The simple present tense and the present continuous: usage and common errors **GRAMMAR BOOSTER** • Extra practice

11 **Past Events** page 88	• Tell someone about a past event
	• Describe past activities
	• Talk about outdoor activities
		• Past-time expressions
		• Outdoor activities
		VOCABULARY BOOSTER
		• More outdoor activities
			• The past tense of <u>be</u>:
			  ◦ Statements, questions, and contractions
			• The simple past tense
			  ◦ Regular verbs, irregular verbs
			  ◦ Statements, questions, and short answers
			GRAMMAR BOOSTER • Extra practice

12 **Appearance and Health** page 96	• Describe appearance • Show concern about an injury • Suggest a remedy	• Adjectives to describe hair • The face • Parts of the body • Accidents and injuries • Ailments, remedies **VOCABULARY BOOSTER** • More parts of the body	• Describing people with <u>be</u> and <u>have</u> • <u>Should</u> + base form for advice **GRAMMAR BOOSTER** • Extra practice
13 **Abilities and Requests** page 104	• Express a wish • Politely decline an invitation • Ask for and agree to do a favor	• Abilities • Adverbs <u>well</u> and <u>badly</u> • Reasons for not doing something • Favors **VOCABULARY BOOSTER** • More musical instruments	• <u>Can</u> and <u>can't</u> for ability • <u>Too</u> + adjective, common errors • Polite requests with <u>Could you</u> + base form **GRAMMAR BOOSTER** • Extra practice

14 **Life Events and Plans** page 112
 	
Units 8–14 Review page 120
	• Get to know someone's life story
	• Discuss plans
	• Express wishes for the future
		• Some life events
		• Academic subjects
		• Leisure activities
		• Life cycle events
		VOCABULARY BOOSTER
		• More academic subjects
		• More leisure activities
			• <u>Be going to</u> + base form
			• <u>Would like</u> + infinitive:
			  ◦ Statements
			  ◦ Questions
			  ◦ Short answers
			  ◦ Contractions
			GRAMMAR BOOSTER • Extra practice

Countries and nationalities / Numbers 100 to 1,000,000,000 / Irregular verbs / Pronunciation table ....page 125
Vocabulary Booster ....page 126
Grammar Booster ....page 136

Conversation Strategies	Listening / Pronunciation	Reading / Writing
• Use Really? to introduce contradictory information • Respond positively to a description with Sounds nice! • Use Actually to introduce an opinion that might surprise • Say I don't know. I'm not sure to avoid making a direct negative statement	**Listening task:** • Determine the best house or apartment for clients of a real estate company • Complete statements about locations of furniture and appliances **Pronunciation:** • Linking sounds	**Reading Texts:** • House and apartment rental listings • Descriptions of people and their homes **Writing Task:** • Compare and contrast your home with homes in a complex illustration
• Use Hi and Hey to greet people informally • Say No kidding! to show surprise • Answer the phone with Hello? • Identify yourself with This is ___ on the phone • Use Well, actually to begin an excuse • Say Oh, I'm sorry after interrupting • Say Talk to you later to indicate the end of a phone conversation	**Listening task:** • Determine weather and temperatures in cities in a weather report • Complete statements about people's activities, using the present continuous **Pronunciation:** • Rising and falling intonation of yes / no and information questions	**Reading Texts:** • A daily planner • A newspaper column about activities in a town **Writing Task:** • Write about plans for the week, using the present continuous
• Say I'll check to indicate you'll get information for someone • Decline an offer politely with No, thanks • Use Please pass the ... to ask for something at the table • Say Here you go as you offer something • Say Nice to see you to greet someone you already know • Use You too to repeat a greeting politely	**Listening task:** • Identify the foods discussed in conversations **Pronunciation:** • Vowel sounds: /i/, /ɪ/, /eɪ/, /ɛ/, /æ/	**Reading Texts:** • Recipe cards • A weekly schedule **Writing Task:** • Write about what you eat in a typical day
• Ask why? to ask for a clearer explanation • Use What about ___? to ask for more information • Use just to minimize the importance of an action • Use a double question to clarify • Say Let me think to gain time to answer • Say Oh yeah to indicate you just remembered something	**Listening task:** • Circle the year you hear • Infer the correct day or month • Choose activities mentioned in conversations **Pronunciation:** • Simple past tense regular verb endings	**Reading Text:** • A blog in which people describe what they did the previous weekend **Writing Tasks:** • Write about the activities of two people, based on a complex picture • Write about your weekend and what you did
• Use Oh to indicate you've understood • Say I'm sorry to hear that, Oh, no, and That's too bad to express sympathy • Use What's wrong? to ask about an illness • Use really to intensify advice with should • Respond to good advice with Good idea • Say I hope you feel better when someone feels sick	**Listening task:** • Identify the people described in conversations • Complete statements about injuries • Identify the ailments and remedies suggested in conversations **Pronunciation** • More vowel sounds	**Reading Text:** • A magazine article about two personalities **Writing Task:** • Write a description of someone you know
• Use I wish I could . . . to express a wish • Use But to introduce contrasting information • Suggest a shared course of action with Let's • Politely decline a suggestion with I'm really sorry but and a reason • Accept a refusal with Maybe some other time • Use Sure and No problem to agree to someone's request for a favor	**Listening task:** • Complete requests for favors **Pronunciation** • Assimilation of sounds: Could you	**Reading Text:** • A journal article about infant-toddler development **Writing Task:** • Describe things people can and can't do when they get old
• Use Not really to soften a negative response • Ask What do you mean? to request clarification • Use Well to explain or clarify • Use emphatic stress on and to indicate two answers	**Listening task:** • Choose correct statements • Circle correct words or phrases • Complete statements about activities, using the present continuous • Infer people's wishes for the future and complete statements, using would like **Pronunciation** • Diphthongs	**Reading Text:** • A short biography of Harry Houdini **Writing Task:** • Write your own illustrated life story, including plans and wishes for the future

Top Notch Pop Lyrics..page 147
ActiveBook Self-Study Disk ....Inside back cover

To the Teacher

What is Top Notch?

Top Notch is a six-level* communicative course that prepares adults and young adults to interact successfully and confidently with both native and non-native speakers of English.

The goal of the *Top Notch* course is to make English unforgettable through:

- ▶ Multiple exposures to new language
- ▶ Numerous opportunities to practice it
- ▶ Deliberate and intensive recycling

The *Top Notch* course has two beginning levels: *Top Notch* Fundamentals for true beginners and *Top Notch* 1 for false beginners.

Each full level of *Top Notch* contains enough material for 60 to 90 hours of classroom instruction. A wide choice of supplementary components makes it easy to tailor *Top Notch* to the needs of your classes.

Summit 1 and *Summit* 2 are the titles of the fifth and sixth levels of the *Top Notch* course. All Student's Books are available in split editions with bound-in workbooks.

The Top Notch instructional design

Daily confirmation of progress

Each easy-to-follow two-page lesson begins with a clearly stated communication goal. All lesson activities are integrated with the goal and systematically build toward a final speaking activity in which students demonstrate achievement of the goal. "Can-do" statements in each unit ensure students' awareness of the continuum of their progress.

A purposeful conversation syllabus

Memorable conversation models provide essential and practical social language that students can carry "in their pockets" for use in real life. Guided conversation pair work enables students to modify, personalize, and extend each model so they can use it to communicate their own thoughts and needs. Free discussion activities are carefully crafted so students can continually retrieve and use the language from the models. All conversation models are informed by the Longman Corpus of Spoken American English.

An emphasis on cultural fluency

Recognizing that English is a global language, *Top Notch* actively equips students to interact socially with people from a variety of cultures and deliberately prepares them to understand accented speakers from diverse language backgrounds.

Intensive vocabulary development

Students actively work with a rich vocabulary of high-frequency words, collocations, and expressions in all units of the Student's Book. Clear illustrations and definitions clarify meaning and provide support for independent study, review, and test preparation. Systematic recycling promotes smooth and continued acquisition of vocabulary from the beginning to the advanced levels of the course.

A dynamic approach to grammar

An explicit grammar syllabus is supported by charts containing clear grammar rules, relevant examples, and explanations of meaning and use. Numerous grammar exercises provide focused practice, and grammar usage is continually activated in communication exercises that illustrate the grammar being learned.

A dedicated pronunciation syllabus

Focused pronunciation, rhythm, and intonation practice is included in each unit, providing application of each pronunciation point to the target language of the unit and facilitating comprehensible pronunciation.

ActiveBook

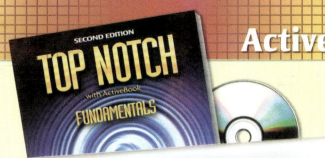

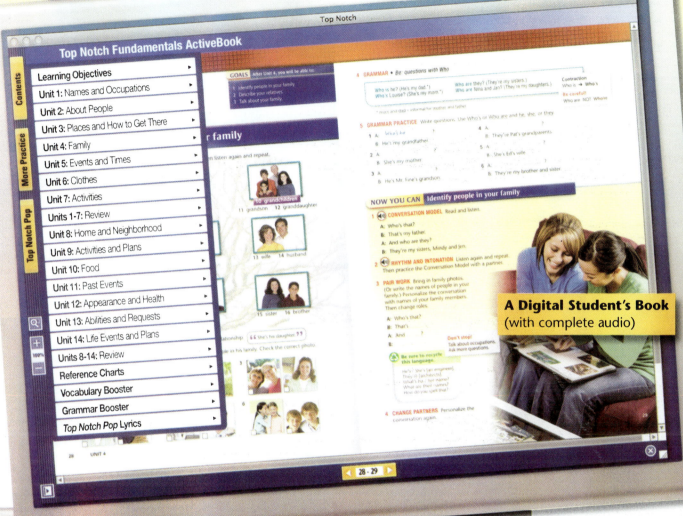

A Digital Student's Book (with complete audio)

Printable test preparation and review

Interactive practice (with daily activity records)
- Extra listening and reading comprehension
- Record-yourself speaking
- Grammar and vocabulary practice
- Games and puzzles
- Top Notch Pop

The Teacher's Edition and Lesson Planner

Includes:
- A bound-in Methods Handbook for professional development
- Detailed lesson plans with suggested teaching times
- Language, culture, and corpus notes
- Student's Book and Workbook answer keys
- Audioscripts
- *Top Notch TV* teaching notes

▶ **ActiveTeach**
- A Digital Student's Book with interactive whiteboard (IWB) software
- Instantly accessible audio and *Top Notch TV* video
- Interactive exercises from the Student's *ActiveBook* for in-class use
- A complete menu of printable extension activities

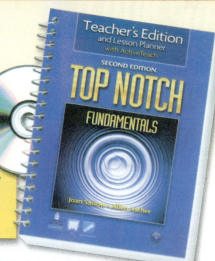

Top Notch TV
A hilarious situation comedy, authentic unrehearsed on-the-street interviews, and *Top Notch Pop* karaoke.

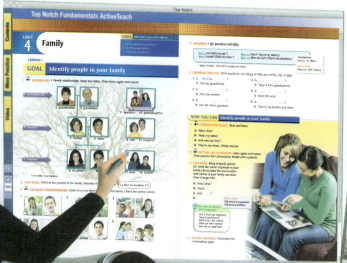

The Digital Student's Book
With zoom, write, highlight, save and other IWB tools.

Printable Extension Activities
Including:
- Writing process worksheets
- Vocabulary flashcards
- Learning strategies
- Graphic organizers
- Pronunciation activities
- Video activity worksheets
  and more . . .

Other components

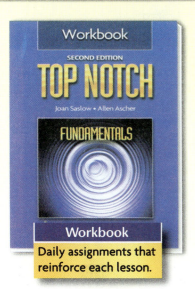

Workbook
Daily assignments that reinforce each lesson.

Classroom Audio Program
Includes a variety of authentic regional and non-native accents.

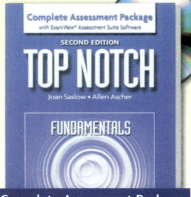

Complete Assessment Package
Ready-made achievement tests. Software provides option to edit, delete, or add items.

Full-Course Placement Tests
Choose printable or online version.

Copy & Go
Board games, role plays, information gaps, and "find someone who. . ." for every lesson.

MyTopNotchLab

An optional online learning tool with:

- ▶ An interactive *Top Notch* Workbook
- ▶ Speaking and writing activities
- ▶ Pop-up grammar help
- ▶ Student's Book *Grammar Booster* exercises
- ▶ *Top Notch TV* with extensive viewing activities
- ▶ Automatically-graded achievement tests
- ▶ Easy course management and record-keeping

Welcome to Top Notch!

GOALS After this unit, you will be able to:
1. Introduce yourself.
2. Greet people.
3. Say good-bye.

GOAL Introduce yourself

1 CONVERSATION MODEL Read and listen.

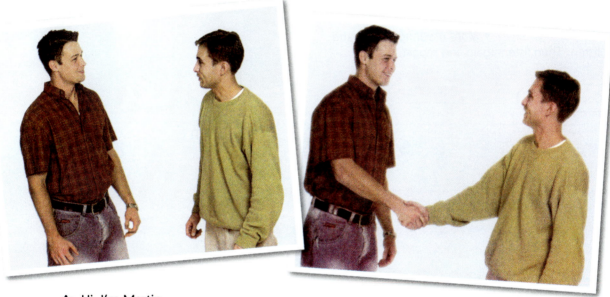

A: Hi. I'm Martin.
B: Hi, Martin. I'm Ben.

A: Nice to meet you, Ben.
B: Nice to meet you, too.

2 RHYTHM AND INTONATION Listen again and repeat. Then practice the Conversation Model with a partner.

NOW YOU CAN Introduce yourself

PAIR WORK Now introduce yourself to your classmates.

Greetings
Hi.
Hello.
I'm [Lisa].

Responses
Nice to meet you.
Glad to meet you.
It's a pleasure to meet you.

GOAL Greet people

1 🔊 **CONVERSATION MODEL** Read and listen.

A: Hi, Len. How are you?
B: Fine, thanks. And you?
A: I'm fine.

2 🔊 **RHYTHM AND INTONATION** Listen again and repeat. Then practice the Conversation Model with a partner.

3 🔊 **VOCABULARY** • *More greetings* Read and listen. Then listen again and repeat.

1 Good morning. 8:00 A.M.

2 Good afternoon. 2:00 P.M.

3 Good evening. 6:00 P.M.

NOW YOU CAN Greet people

PAIR WORK Now greet your classmates.

🔊 **Greetings**
How are you?
How's everything?
How's it going?

🔊 **Responses**
☐ { Fine. / I'm fine.
    Great.
☐ { Not bad.
    So-so.

Welcome

GOAL Say good-bye

1 🔊 **CONVERSATION MODEL** Read and listen.

A: Good-bye, Charlotte.
B: Good-bye, Emily.
A: See you tomorrow.
B: OK. See you!

2 🔊 **RHYTHM AND INTONATION** Listen again and repeat. Then practice the Conversation Model with a partner.

NOW YOU CAN Say good-bye

PAIR WORK Now say good-bye to your classmates.

🔊 **Ways to say good-bye**
Good-bye.
Bye.
See you later.
Take care.

NOW I CAN... ✓
☐ Introduce myself.
☐ Greet people.
☐ Say good-bye.

3

UNIT 1
Names and Occupations

GOALS After Unit 1, you will be able to:
1. Tell a classmate your occupation.
2. Identify your classmates.
3. Spell names.

LESSON 1

GOAL Tell a classmate your occupation

1 🔊 **VOCABULARY** • *Occupations* Read and listen. Then listen again and repeat.

1 a teacher

2 a student

3 an architect

4 an actor

5 an athlete

6 a musician

7 an artist

8 a banker

9 a singer

10 a flight attendant

VOCABULARY BOOSTER
More occupations • p. 126

2 PAIR WORK Say the name of an occupation. Your partner points (☞) to the picture.

3 GRAMMAR • *Verb be: singular statements / Contractions*

Affirmative statements / Contractions	Negative statements / Contractions
I **am** Ann. / I**'m** Ann.	I **am not** Jen. / I**'m not** Jen.
You **are** an architect. / You**'re** an architect.	You **are not** an artist. / You**'re not** an artist. / You **aren't** an artist.
He **is** a teacher. / He**'s** a teacher.	He **is not** a student. / He**'s not** a student. / He **isn't** a student.
She **is** a nurse. / She**'s** a nurse.	She **is not** a banker. / She**'s not** a banker. / She **isn't** a banker.

Articles a / an
a teacher
an actor

4 UNIT 1

4 **GRAMMAR PRACTICE** Write the article a or an for each occupation.

1 .... architect   3 .... banker   5 .... singer
2 .... student   4 .... musician 6 .... athlete

5 **PAIR WORK** Point to the people on page 4. Say He's ___ or She's ___ .

" He's a teacher. "

" She's a flight attendant. "

6 **INTEGRATED PRACTICE** Read the names and occupations. Write affirmative and negative statements.

1 Matt Damon *He's an actor. He's not an architect.*   3 Hee-Young Lim ....
2 Carlos Vives ....   4 Constantina Tomescu ....

NOW YOU CAN Tell a classmate your occupation

1 🔊 **CONVERSATION MODEL** Read and listen.

A: What do you do?
B: I'm an architect. And you?
A: I'm a banker.

2 🔊 **RHYTHM AND INTONATION** Listen again and repeat. Then practice the Conversation Model with a partner.

3 **PAIR WORK** Personalize the conversation. Use your own occupations.

A: What do you do?
B: I'm .... And you?
A: I'm ....

4 **CHANGE PARTNERS** Tell another classmate your occupation.

LESSON 2

GOAL Identify your classmates

1 🔊 **VOCABULARY** • *More occupations* Read and listen. Then listen again and repeat.

1 She's **a chef**.

2 He's **a writer**.

3 She's **a manager**.

4 She's **a scientist**.

5 He's **a doctor**.

6 She's **an engineer**.

7 He's **a photographer**.

8 He's **a pilot**.

2 GRAMMAR • *Singular and plural nouns / Be: plural statements*

Singular nouns	Plural nouns
a chef	2 chefs
an athlete	3 athletes

Subject pronouns

Singular	Plural
I	we
you	you
he	they
she	

Affirmative statements / Contractions
We **are** photographers. / We**'re** photographers.
You **are** scientists. / You**'re** scientists.
They **are** writers. / They**'re** writers.

Negative statements / Contractions
We **are not** chefs. / We**'re not** chefs. / We **aren't** chefs.
You **are not** pilots. / You**'re not** pilots. / You **aren't** pilots.
They **are not** artists. / They**'re not** artists. / They **aren't** artists.

3 GRAMMAR PRACTICE Complete each statement with a singular or plural form of <u>be</u>.

1 I .... a writer.
2 She .... not a pilot.
3 We .... doctors.
4 They .... not scientists.
5 We .... managers.

4 INTEGRATED PRACTICE Circle the correct word or words to complete each statement.

1 I am (an artist / artists / artist).
2 We are (a flight attendant / flight attendants / flight attendant).
3 She is (banker / a banker / bankers).
4 They are (a writer / writers / writer).

5 GRAMMAR • Be: yes / no questions and short answers

Yes / no questions	Short answers	
Are you / Is he / Is Tanya } an architect?	Yes, I am. / Yes, {he/she} is.	No, I'm not. / No, {he's/she's} not.
Are you / Are they / Are Ted and Jane } musicians?	Yes, {we/they} are.	No, {we're/they're} not.

Be careful!
Yes, I am.   NOT ~~Yes, I'm.~~
Yes, she is.   NOT ~~Yes, she's.~~
Yes, we are.   NOT ~~Yes, we're.~~

6 GRAMMAR PRACTICE Complete the conversations. Use contractions when possible.

1. A: ...Are... they Abby and Jonah?
   B: Yes, ...
2. A: .... she Hanna?
   B: No, ... Ella.
3. A: .... you Rachel and Philip?
   B: No, we'.......... . ... Judith and Jack.
4. A: .... a chef?
   B: Yes, I ....
5. A: .... he Evan?
   B: No, ... not. He'.......... Michael.
6. A: Is .... Tim?
   B: ...., he'.......... . He's Louis.

7 PAIR WORK Practice the conversations from Exercise 6.

8 PAIR WORK Ask your partner two questions. Answer your partner's questions.

"Are you an artist?"
"Yes, I am."

NOW YOU CAN Identify your classmates

1 CONVERSATION MODEL Read and listen.
A: Excuse me. Are you Marie?
B: No, I'm not. I'm Laura. That's Marie.
A: Where?
B: Right over there.
A: Thank you.
B: You're welcome.

2 RHYTHM AND INTONATION Listen again and repeat. Then practice the Conversation Model with a partner.

3 PAIR WORK Personalize the conversation. Use real names. Then change roles.
A: Excuse me. Are you ....?
B: No, I'm not. I'm .... That's ....
A: Where?
B: Right over there.
A: Thank you.
B: You're welcome.

4 CHANGE PARTNERS Identify other classmates.

LESSON 3

GOAL Spell names

1 🔊 **VOCABULARY** • *The alphabet* Read and listen. Then listen again and repeat.

A B C D E F G H I J K L M
N O P Q R S T U V W X Y Z

2 🔊 **LISTENING COMPREHENSION** Listen. Circle the letter you hear.

1. A K   4. U O   7. F X   10. J G   13. D G
2. B E   5. B Z   8. X S   11. L N   14. H K
3. M N   6. T C   9. Z V   12. K J   15. P E

3 PAIR WORK Read 10 letters aloud to your partner. Point to the letters you hear.

L W V G S
J C F I Y Q
P X B K H
R M U O N
E T A D Z

4 🔊 **LISTENING COMPREHENSION** Listen. Circle the correct spelling. Then spell each name aloud.

1	Green	Greene	Grin
2	Leigh	Lee	Li
3	Katharine	Katherine	Catharine

5 🔊 **LISTENING COMPREHENSION** Listen to the conversations. Write the names.

1 ....
2 ....
3 ....

6 GRAMMAR • *Proper nouns and common nouns*

Capital letters
A B C
Lowercase letters
a b c

Proper nouns
The names of people and places are proper nouns. Use a capital letter to begin a proper noun.
  Melanie Pepper   New Delhi   Nicaragua

Common nouns
Other nouns are common nouns. Use a lowercase letter to begin a common noun.
  morning   doctor   student

7 GRAMMAR PRACTICE Circle the proper nouns. Underline the common nouns.

1 Mary Chase 3 name 5 partners
2 letter 4 France 6 alphabet

8 GRAMMAR PRACTICE Check ✓ the common nouns. Capitalize the proper nouns.

☐ 1 marie (M) ☐ 3 sarah browne ☐ 5 canada ☐ 7 letter
☑ 2 partner ☐ 4 teacher ☐ 6 noun ☐ 8 grammar

9 PRONUNCIATION • *Syllables* Read and listen. Then listen again and repeat.

1 syllable	2 syllables	3 syllables	4 syllables
chef	bank • er	ar • chi • tect	pho • tog • ra • pher

10 PAIR WORK First, take turns saying each word. Write the number of syllables. Then listen to check your work.

1 teacher .... 3 vocabulary .... 5 occupation ....
2 students .... 4 alphabet .... 6 they're ....

NOW YOU CAN Spell names

1 CONVERSATION MODEL Read and listen.

A: Hello. I'm John Bello.
B: Excuse me?
A: John Bello.
B: How do you spell that?
A: B-E-L-L-O.
B: Thanks!

2 RHYTHM AND INTONATION Listen again and repeat. Then practice the Conversation Model with a partner.

3 PAIR WORK Personalize the conversation. Use your own name. Then change roles.

A: Hello. I'm ....
B: Excuse me?
A: ....
B: How do you spell that?
A: ....
B: Thanks!

Don't stop!
Ask about occupations. "What do you do?"

4 CHANGE PARTNERS Personalize the conversation again.

Extension

More Practice
ActiveBook *Self-Study Disc*

grammar · vocabulary · listening
reading · speaking · pronunciation

1:28
1 🔊 LISTENING COMPREHENSION Listen to the conversations. Write the number of the conversation in the boxes.

1:29
2 🔊 LISTENING COMPREHENSION Listen to the conversations. Complete the information.

3 PAIR WORK Choose a famous person. Write that person's information on the form. Then play the role of that person and introduce "yourself" to your partner.

NAME:
OCCUPATION:

"Hi. I'm Sean Penn. I'm an actor. And you?"

4 INTEGRATED PRACTICE Answer the questions about four famous people. Use subject pronouns and contractions.

Denzel Washington
actor

Tania Libertad
singer

Se Ri Pak
athlete

Gabriel García Márquez
writer

GRAMMAR BOOSTER
Extra practice • p.136

1 Is Denzel Washington an actor or a singer?
   He's an actor.

2 What's Tania Libertad's occupation?
   ....

3 Is Se Ri Pak a teacher?
   ....

4 Are Se Ri Pak and Gabriel García Márquez scientists?
   ....

5 What's Gabriel García Márquez's occupation?
   ....

6 Is Se Ri Pak an athlete?
   ....

5 PERSONAL RESPONSES Write responses with real information.

1 "Hi. I'm Art Potter."
   YOU ....

2 "Are you a teacher?"
   YOU ....

3 "What do you do?"
   YOU ....

4 "Thank you."
   YOU ....

1:30/1:31
Top Notch Pop
"What Do You Do?" Lyrics p. 147

Review

POINT Name the occupations in the pictures. For example:
She's an artist.

PAIR WORK

1 Ask and answer questions about the people. For example:
Is John a photographer? Yes, he is.

2 Create conversations for the people. For example:
Hi. I'm ___.

WRITING Write affirmative and negative statements about the people in the picture. For example:
Rose is an artist. She's not an architect.

NOW I CAN...
- ☐ Tell a classmate my occupation.
- ☐ Identify my classmates.
- ☐ Spell names.

UNIT 2
About People

GOALS After Unit 2, you will be able to:
1 Introduce people.
2 Tell someone your first and last name.
3 Get someone's contact information.

LESSON 1
GOAL Introduce people

1 🔊 **VOCABULARY** • *Relationships* Read and listen. Then listen again and repeat.

1 a classmate

2 a friend

3 a neighbor

4 a boss

5 a colleague

VOCABULARY BOOSTER
More relationships • p. 127

2 GRAMMAR • *Possessive nouns and adjectives*

Possessive nouns
Al Smith is **Kate's** boss.
Larry's colleague is Teresa.
We are **Sara and Todd's** neighbors.
I am **Ms. Tan's** student.
We are **Marty's** classmates.

Possessive adjectives
He is **her** boss.
Teresa is **his** colleague.
We are **their** neighbors.
She is **my** teacher.
Marty is **our** classmate.

Ms. Ellis is **Joe's** teacher.
Joe is **her** student.

Subject pronouns	Possessive adjectives
I →	my
you →	your
he →	his
she →	her
we →	our
they →	their

3 GRAMMAR PRACTICE Circle the correct word or words to complete each sentence.

1 Mr. Thomas is (**my** / I) boss.
2 Is Mrs. Cory (you / **your**) teacher?
3 Is (she / **her**) Dr. Kim?
4 Are (**they** / their) Connie and Sam?
5 Are (**your** / you) Barry's friend?
6 He's (**my** / I) colleague.
7 Mr. Bello is (Alec / **Alec's**) neighbor.
8 Jake is (Ms. Rose / **Ms. Rose's**) student.
9 (He's / **His**) an architect.
10 (**Kyle** / Kyle's) and Ray's new classmate is Gail.

4 PAIR WORK Tell a classmate about at least three of your relationships. Use the Vocabulary.

> ❝ Jerry is my classmate. Ted and Jan Keyes are my neighbors. ❞

5 🔊 **LISTENING COMPREHENSION** Listen to the conversations. Write the relationships.

1 Bruce is her ....
2 Patty is his ....
3 Mr. Grant is her ....
4 Rob is her ....
5 Carlos is his ....

6 **GRAMMAR** • *Be from* / Questions with *Where*

> I'm from Toronto.

Are you from Paraguay?
Is she from Moscow?

Where are you from?
Where's she from?

Be careful! Are you from Spain?
Yes, I am. NOT Yes, I'm from.

Yes, I am. / No, I'm not.
Yes, she is. / No, she's not.

We're from Bangkok.
She's from Canada.

Contractions
Where is → Where's
Where are NOT Where're

7 **GRAMMAR PRACTICE** Complete the conversations with *be from*. Use contractions when possible.

1 A: ..Where's.. your neighbor .... ?
   B: She .... Canada.

2 A: .... they .... ?
   B: .... Paris.

3 A: .... your boss .... ?
   B: He .... Fortaleza.

4 A: .... you and your friend .... ?
   B: .... Pusan.

NOW YOU CAN | Introduce people

1 🔊 **CONVERSATION MODEL** Read and listen.

A: Tom, this is Paula. Paula's my classmate.
B: Hi, Paula.
C: Hi, Tom. Nice to meet you.
B: Nice to meet you, too.

2 🔊 **RHYTHM AND INTONATION** Listen again and repeat. Then practice the Conversation Model with a partner.

3 **GROUP WORK** Personalize the conversation. Introduce classmates. Use your own names. Then change roles.

A: ...., this is .... 's my ....
B: Hi, ...
C: Hi, ... Nice to meet you.
B: Nice to meet you, too.

 Be sure to recycle this language.

Don't stop!
Ask questions.

Where are you from?
What do you do?

4 **CHANGE PARTNERS** Introduce other classmates.

LESSON 2

GOAL Tell someone your first and last name

1 🔊 **VOCABULARY** • *Titles and names* Read and listen. Then listen again and repeat.

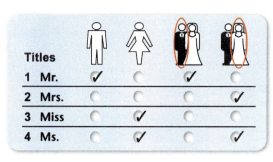

Mr. Charles Lee   Mrs. Vivian Lee
5 first name   6 last name

VOCABULARY BOOSTER
More titles • p. 127

Be careful!
Mr. Charles Lee OR Mr. Lee
Mrs. Vivian Lee OR Mrs. Lee
NOT ~~Mr. Charles~~
NOT ~~Mrs. Vivian~~

2 PAIR WORK Introduce yourself to a classmate. Use a title and your last name.

"Hi. I'm Mr. Wilson."

"Nice to meet you, Mr. Wilson."

3 🔊 **LISTENING COMPREHENSION** Listen. Circle the correct information. Then listen again and check your answers.

1
[X] Mr.
[ ] Mrs.   Alex   Davis
[ ] Miss   first name   last name
[ ] Ms.

2
[ ] Mr.
[ ] Mrs.   Nancy   Sullivan
[ ] Miss   first name   last name
[X] Ms.

3
[X] Mr.
[ ] Mrs.   Frank   Sun
[ ] Miss   first name   last name
[ ] Ms.

4
[ ] Mr.
[X] Mrs.   Wendy   Roberts
[ ] Miss   first name   last name
[ ] Ms.

[X] Mr.
[ ] Mrs.   Fred   Roberts
[ ] Miss   first name   last name
[ ] Ms.

5
[ ] Mr.
[ ] Mrs.   RITA   OLIVEIRA
[ ] Miss   first name   last name
[X] Ms.

6
[ ] Mr.
[ ] Mrs.   Pam   García
[ ] Miss   first name   last name
[X] Ms.

[X] Mr.
[ ] Mrs.   Henry   Solas
[ ] Miss   first name   last name
[ ] Ms.

4 VOCABULARY PRACTICE Fill out the forms. Check or circle the correct titles.

You:

☐ Mr. ☐ Mrs. ☐ Miss ☐ Ms.

_____ _____
first name   last name

A classmate:

☐ Mr.
☐ Mrs.   first name
☐ Miss
☐ Ms.   last name

Your teacher:

☐ Mr. ☐ Mrs. ☐ Miss ☐ Ms.

_____ _____
first name   last name

NOW YOU CAN Tell someone your first and last name

1 CONVERSATION MODEL Read and listen.

A: What's your last name, please?
B: Fava.
A: And your first name?
B: My first name? Bob.

A: Thank you, Mr. Fava.
B: You're welcome.

2 RHYTHM AND INTONATION Listen again and repeat. Then practice the Conversation Model with a partner.

3 PAIR WORK Personalize the conversation. Use your own names. Write your partner's information on the form. Then change roles.

A: What's your last name, please?
B: ....
A: And your first name?
B: My first name? ....
A: Thank you, ...
B: You're welcome.

Mr.
Mrs. _____ _____
Miss   first name   last name
Ms.

Don't stop! Ask more questions.

♻ Be sure to recycle this language.
How do you spell that?
What do you do?
Where are you from?

4 CHANGE PARTNERS Personalize the conversation again.

LESSON 3

GOAL Get someone's contact information

1 🔊 **VOCABULARY** • *Numbers 0 – 20* Read and listen. Then listen again and repeat.

0 zero	7 seven	14 fourteen
1 one	8 eight	15 fifteen
2 two	9 nine	16 sixteen
3 three	10 ten	17 seventeen
4 four	11 eleven	18 eighteen
5 five	12 twelve	19 nineteen
6 six	13 thirteen	20 twenty

2 **PAIR WORK** Read a number aloud from the picture. Your partner writes the number on a separate sheet of paper.

3 **GRAMMAR** • *Be: information questions with What*

What's his name?	(Mark Crandall.)
What's his last name?	(Crandall.)
What's Ellen's address?	(18 Main Street.)
What's her e-mail address?	(Dover14@hipnet.com.)
What's their phone number?	(835-555-0037.)
What are their first names?	(Luis and Samuel.)

What is → What's

How to say e-mail addresses and phone numbers:
Say "dover fourteen **at** hipnet **dot** com."
Say "oh" for *zero*: 0037 = "oh-oh-three-seven."

4 🔊 **PRONUNCIATION** • *Stress in two-word pairs* Read and listen. Then listen again and repeat.

first name   **phone** num ber   **e**-mail address

5 🔊 **LISTENING COMPREHENSION** Listen to the conversations. Write the information. Then listen again and check your work.

	NAME		PHONE NUMBER	E-MAIL
1	Valerie	Peterson	___-___-____	_____@_____
2	Mathilda		___-___-____	
3		Quinn	___-___-____	_____@_____
4	Joseph		___-___-____	

16 UNIT 2

6 INTEGRATED PRACTICE Complete the questions.

1 A: *What's his* address?
B: 11 Main Street.

2 A: .... phone number?
B: 22-63-140.

3 A: .... address?
B: 18 Bank Street.

4 A: .... phone number?
B: 878-456-0055.

5 A: .... e-mail address?
B: It's sgast@mp.net.

6 A: .... phone number?
B: 44-78-35.

NOW YOU CAN Get someone's contact information

1 🔊 **CONVERSATION MODEL** Read and listen. (1:43)

A: What's your name?
B: Dave Mitchell.
A: And what's your phone number?
B: 523-6620.
A: 523-6620?
B: That's right.

2 🔊 **RHYTHM AND INTONATION** Listen again and repeat. Then practice the Conversation Model with a partner. (1:44)

3 **PAIR WORK** Personalize the conversation. Write your partner's answers on a separate sheet of paper. Then change roles.

A: What's your ....?
B: ....
A: And what's your phone number?
B: ....
A: ....?
B: That's right.

Don't stop!
Continue the conversation.
Ask more questions.

 Be sure to recycle this language.

first name / last name
address / e-mail address
Thank you.
You're welcome.
Nice to meet you.
Good-bye.

4 **CHANGE PARTNERS** Get other classmates' contact information.

Extension

More Practice
ActiveBook Self-Study Disc

grammar • vocabulary • listening
reading • speaking • pronunciation

1 🔊 **READING** Read about six famous people. Where are they from?

This is Frank Gehry. Where is Mr. Gehry from? He's from Canada. And what's his occupation? He's an architect.

This is Paco de Lucía, from Spain. What's his occupation? He's a musician.

This is Maria Sharapova. She's from Russia. What's Ms. Sharapova's occupation? She's an athlete.

This is John Travolta. Mr. Travolta has two occupations. He's an actor and a pilot. He's from the United States.

This is Banana Yoshimoto. Ms. Yoshimoto is from Japan. What's her occupation? She's a writer.

2 PAIR WORK Ask and answer questions about people in the Reading. Use the verb <u>be</u>.

❝ Is Frank Gehry a doctor? ❞

❝ Is Maria Sharapova from the United States? ❞

❝ Where's Mr. Travolta from? ❞

On your *ActiveBook* Self-Study Disc:
Extra Reading Comprehension Questions

3 SPEAKING Point to the people in the photos. Ask your partner questions about their contact information.

Ryan Hale
🏠 12 Bank St.
✉ rhale@ccc.com

Norma Chin
☎ 33-55-0078
✉ nchin@hipnet.com

Fran Green   Bill Green
☎ 34-67-9899
🏠 13 Quinn St.

GRAMMAR BOOSTER
Extra practice • p.137

Top Notch Pop
"Excuse Me, Please"   Lyrics p. 147

Review

PERSONAL INFORMATION

First name: _____   Last name: _____
Address: _____
Phone: _____   e-mail: _____

PAIR WORK

1 Create a conversation for the people in the first picture. Complete the form with your partner's information. Start like this:
   What's your ___?

2 Create a conversation for the people in the second picture. Introduce the two women. Start like this:
   This is ___. She's my ___.

WRITING Write sentences about your relationships. For example:

Nancy Lee is my friend. She's from Vancouver.
She's a ...

NOW I CAN... ✓
☐ Introduce people.
☐ Tell someone my first and last name.
☐ Get someone's contact information.

UNIT 3

Places and How to Get There

GOALS After Unit 3, you will be able to:
1. Talk about locations.
2. Discuss how to get places.
3. Discuss transportation.

LESSON 1

GOAL Talk about locations

1 🔊 **VOCABULARY** • *Places in the neighborhood* Read and listen. Then listen again and repeat.

1 a pharmacy

2 a restaurant

3 a bank

4 a school

5 a newsstand

6 a bookstore

VOCABULARY BOOSTER
More places • p. 127

2 🔊 **LISTENING COMPREHENSION** Listen. Write the places you hear.

1 .... 3 ....
2 .... 4 ....

3 **PAIR WORK** Say the name of a place. Your partner writes the word.

4 🔊 **VOCABULARY** • *Locations* Read and listen. Then listen again and repeat.

1 across the street

2 down the street

3 around the corner

4 on the left

5 on the right

6 next to the bank

7 between the bookstore and the bank

5 PAIR WORK Take turns making statements about the location of the places.

"The bank is across the street."

    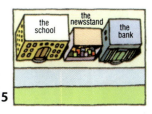

1 2 3 4 5

6 GRAMMAR • *Be*: questions with *Where* / Subject pronoun *it*

Ask questions with *Where* for locations.
  Where's the restaurant?

Use *it* to replace the names of places.
  It's down the street. (*It* = the restaurant)

Contractions
Where is → Where's
It is → It's

1:51
7 PRONUNCIATION • *Falling intonation for questions with Where* Read and listen. Then listen again and repeat.

1 Where is it?
2 Where's the bank?
3 Where's the school?
4 Where's the newsstand?

NOW YOU CAN | Talk about locations

1:52
1 CONVERSATION MODEL Read and listen.

A: Excuse me. Where's the bank?
B: The bank? It's around the corner.
A: Thanks!
B: You're welcome.

1:53
2 RHYTHM AND INTONATION Listen again and repeat. Then practice the Conversation Model with a partner.

3 PAIR WORK Find the people on the map. Talk about the location of places on the map. Then change roles.

A: Excuse me. Where's the ………?
B: ………? It's ……… .
A: Thanks!
B: You're welcome.

4 CHANGE PARTNERS Ask about other locations.

LESSON 2

GOAL Discuss how to get places

1 🔊 **VOCABULARY** • *Ways to get places* Read and listen. Then listen again and repeat.

1 walk   2 drive   3 take a taxi   4 take the train   5 take the bus

2 **GRAMMAR** • *The imperative*

Use imperatives to give instructions and directions.
Affirmative imperatives
Drive [to the bank].
Take the bus [to the pharmacy].

Negative imperatives
Don't walk.
Don't take the train.

Do not → Don't

3 **INTEGRATED PRACTICE** Follow the directions.

Partner A: Read a direction.
Partner B: Say the letter of the correct picture.

1 Walk to the bookstore.
2 Don't drive to the restaurant.
3 Take the bus to the bank.
4 Don't walk to the pharmacy.
5 Drive down the street.

Partner B: Read a direction.
Partner A: Say the letter of the correct picture.

6 Take the bus down the street.
7 Don't take the bus to the bank.
8 Walk to the bank.
9 Take a taxi to the restaurant.
10 Drive to the pharmacy.

a   b

c   d

e   f

g   h

 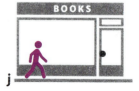
i   j

4 🔊 1:55 **LISTENING COMPREHENSION** Listen. Write the directions. Use an affirmative and a negative imperative.

1. *Take the bus. Don't drive.*
2. ....
3. ....
4. ....
5. ....

NOW YOU CAN | Discuss how to get places

1 🔊 1:56 **CONVERSATION MODEL** Read and listen.

A: Can I walk to the bookstore?
B: The bookstore? Sure.
A: And what about the school?
B: The school? Don't walk. Drive.
A: OK. Thanks!

2 🔊 1:57 **RHYTHM AND INTONATION** Listen again and repeat. Then practice the Conversation Model with a partner.

3 PAIR WORK Change the model. Use the photos below. Ask how to get to places in the neighborhood. Then change roles.

A: Can I walk to the ....?
B: The ....? ....
A: And what about the ....?
B: The ....? Don't ....
A: OK. Thanks!

♻ Be sure to recycle this language.

Where is it?
It's ⎰ across the street.
     ⎮ down the street.
     ⎨ around the corner.
     ⎮ next to the ___.
     ⎱ between the ___ and the ___.

Don't stop!
Ask about locations.

4 CHANGE PARTNERS Discuss more places.

LESSON 3

GOAL Discuss transportation

1 🔊 **VOCABULARY** • *Means of transportation* Read and listen. Then listen again and repeat.

1 a car
2 a bicycle
3 a moped
4 a subway
5 a motorcycle

Also remember:
a bus
a train
a taxi

2 **PAIR WORK** Take turns. Spell a Vocabulary word aloud. Your partner writes the word.

3 **GRAMMAR** • *By to express means*

by taxi   **by** bicycle   **by** motorcycle

4 🔊 **LISTENING COMPREHENSION** Listen. Circle the means of transportation you hear.

1   2   3   4   5

5 🔊 **VOCABULARY** • *Destinations* Read and listen. Then listen again and repeat.

1 go to work

2 go home

3 go to school

6 🔊 **LISTENING COMPREHENSION** Listen. Use a <u>by</u> phrase to write the means of transportation. Then check the box for work, home, or school.

		💼💻	🏠	📖
1	by car	☐	✓	☐
2		☐	☐	☐
3		☐	☐	☐
4		☐	☐	☐
5		☐	☐	☐
6		☐	☐	☐

NOW YOU CAN Discuss transportation

1 🔊 **CONVERSATION MODEL** Read and listen.

    A: How do you go to school?
    B: By subway. What about you?
    A: Me? I walk.

2 🔊 **RHYTHM AND INTONATION** Listen again and repeat. Then practice the Conversation Model with a partner.

3 **PAIR WORK** Personalize the conversation. Ask about work, school, and home. Answer with a <u>by</u> phrase. Then change roles.

    A: How do you go ....?
    B: .... What about you?
    A: Me? I ....

> **Don't stop!**
> Ask about other places.

4 **CHANGE PARTNERS** Personalize the conversation again.

Extension

More Practice
ActiveBook Self-Study Disc

grammar · vocabulary · listening
reading · speaking · pronunciation

1 🔊 1:64 **READING** Read about how people go to work and school.

I'm an engineer. I'm lucky. I can walk to work. My office is around the corner from my home.

I'm a writer from New York. I go to work by subway. I take the subway home, too.

My name is Jasper White. I go to work by train, and I go home by car with my colleague, Dr. Randall Marshall. He's a neighbor down the street from my home.

and this is my teacher, Ms. Clark. I'm a student. My school is right next to my home. I walk to school with my friends. We walk home together, too.

I'm Katie's teacher, but *my* home is not next to our school. Can I walk to school? Definitely not! I take the bus to school, and I go home by train.

2 PAIR WORK Ask and answer the questions.

"Is Jennie Beck a teacher?"

"No, she's not. She's a writer."

1 Is Jasper White a doctor?
2 Is Randall Marshall Dr. White's friend or his colleague?
3 Is Dr. Marshall Dr. White's neighbor?
4 Is Katie Simpson a teacher?
5 What is Katie's teacher's name?
6 Is their school next to Ms. Clark's home?
7 Where is Kim Lee's office?
8 Your own question: .... ?

On your *ActiveBook* Self-Study Disc:
Extra Reading Comprehension Questions

GRAMMAR BOOSTER
Extra practice • p. 138

3 GROUP WORK On the board, make a map of places near your school. Write the names of the places. Then take turns describing the locations of the places.

 Be sure to recycle this language.

Where's the [pharmacy]?
It's ___.
Can I [walk] to the [restaurant]?
Take / Don't take the [bus].

Walk / Don't [drive].
Go by bus.
Don't go by train.

UNIT 4 Family

GOALS After Unit 4, you will be able to:
1. Identify people in your family.
2. Describe your relatives.
3. Talk about your family.

LESSON 1
GOAL: Identify people in your family

1 🔊 **VOCABULARY** • *Family relationships* Read and listen. Then listen again and repeat.

1 grandparents

2 grandmother

3 grandfather

10 grandchildren
11 grandson   12 granddaughter

4 parents

5 mother

6 father

13 wife   14 husband

7 children*

8 daughter

9 son

15 sister   16 brother

*one **child** / two **children**

2 **PAIR WORK** Point to two people in the family. Describe their relationship.   « She's his daughter. »

3 🔊 **LISTENING COMPREHENSION** Listen to a man identify people in his family. Check the correct photo.

1
2
3
4
5
6

4 GRAMMAR • Be: questions with Who

Who is he? (He's my dad.*)
Who's Louise? (She's my mom.*)
Who are they? (They're my sisters.)
Who are Nina and Jan? (They're my daughters.)

Contraction
Who is → Who's

Be careful!
Who are NOT ~~Who're~~

*mom and dad = informal for mother and father

5 GRAMMAR PRACTICE Write questions. Use Who's or Who are and he, she, or they.

1 A: Who's he ?
   B: He's my grandfather.

2 A: .... ?
   B: She's my mother.

3 A: .... ?
   B: He's Mr. Fine's grandson.

4 A: .... ?
   B: They're Pat's grandparents.

5 A: .... ?
   B: She's Ed's wife.

6 A: .... ?
   B: They're my brother and sister.

NOW YOU CAN Identify people in your family

2:04
1 **CONVERSATION MODEL** Read and listen.

A: Who's that?
B: That's my father.
A: And who are they?
B: They're my sisters, Mindy and Jen.

2:05
2 **RHYTHM AND INTONATION** Listen again and repeat. Then practice the Conversation Model with a partner.

3 **PAIR WORK** Bring in family photos. (Or write the names of people in your family.) Personalize the conversation with names of your family members. Then change roles.

A: Who's that?
B: That's ....
A: And .... ?
B: ....

Don't stop!
Talk about occupations.
Ask more questions.

♻ Be sure to recycle this language.

He's / She's [an engineer].
They're [architects].
What's his / her name?
What are their names?
How do you spell that?

4 **CHANGE PARTNERS** Personalize the conversation again.

LESSON 2

GOAL Describe your relatives

1 **VOCABULARY** • *Adjectives to describe people*
Read and listen. Then listen again and repeat.

VOCABULARY BOOSTER
More adjectives • p. 128

1 pretty   2 handsome   4 cute   5 short   6 tall   7 old   8 young

3 good-looking

2 **GRAMMAR** • *Be with adjectives / Adverbs very and so*

Describe people with a form of be and an adjective.
She's pretty.   They're good-looking.
He's handsome.   Your children are cute.

The adverbs very and so make adjectives stronger.
They're very good-looking. She's so pretty!
He's very handsome.   Your children are so cute!

3 **PAIR WORK** Use the Vocabulary to describe two people in your class.

"Gina and Deborah are very pretty."

4 **LISTENING COMPREHENSION** Listen to the conversations.
Circle the adjective that describes each person.

1 Her husband is (handsome / tall / old).
2 His daughter is (tall / good-looking / cute).
3 Her brothers are (tall / good-looking / young).
4 His son is (tall / good-looking / short).
5 Her father is (tall / old / short).
6 His sisters are (tall / good-looking / short).

5 **INTEGRATED PRACTICE** Look at the pictures. Complete each sentence with a form of be and an adjective.

1 Your sisters .... so ....

2 Your daughter .... so ....!

3 Our grandfather .... very ....

30 UNIT 4

4 His fiancée .... very ....

5 His wife .... so .... !

6 Your brother .... so tall. And his colleague .... very ....

6 INTEGRATED PRACTICE Write three sentences about people in your family. Use adjectives and the adverbs <u>very</u> or <u>so</u> to describe the people.

My brother is very tall.

NOW YOU CAN Describe your relatives

1 🔊 2:08 **CONVERSATION MODEL** Read and listen.

A: Tell me about your father.
B: Well, he's a doctor. And he's very tall.
A: And how about your mother?
B: She's a scientist. She's very pretty.

2 🔊 2:09 **RHYTHM AND INTONATION** Listen again and repeat. Then practice the Conversation Model with a partner.

3 PAIR WORK Personalize the conversation. Describe your relatives. Then change roles.

A: Tell me about your ....
B: Well, ... And ....
A: And how about your .... ?
B: ....

Don't stop!
Ask about other people in your partner's family.

4 CHANGE PARTNERS Ask about other classmates' relatives.

LESSON 3

GOAL Talk about your family

1 GRAMMAR • Verb *have* / *has*: affirmative statements

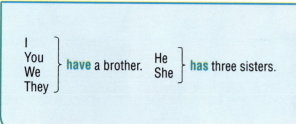

I / You / We / They **have** a brother.   He / She **has** three sisters.

"I **have** one son and one daughter."

2 GRAMMAR PRACTICE Complete the sentences. Use *have* or *has*. Then complete the sentence about your own family.

1 Mark .... two brothers.
2 My grandmother .... five grandsons.
3 They .... a granddaughter.
4 We .... twelve grandchildren.
5 Carl and Anna .... two children.
6 She .... five sisters.
7 They .... no brothers or sisters.
YOU I ....

3 VOCABULARY • Numbers 21–101 Read and listen. Then listen again and repeat.

21 twenty-one	25 twenty-five	29 twenty-nine	40 forty	80 eighty
22 twenty-two	26 twenty-six	30 thirty	50 fifty	90 ninety
23 twenty-three	27 twenty-seven	31 thirty-one	60 sixty	100 one hundred
24 twenty-four	28 twenty-eight	32 thirty-two	70 seventy	101 one hundred one

4 PRONUNCIATION • Numbers Listen and repeat. Then practice saying the numbers on your own.

13 • 30   17 • 70
14 • 40   18 • 80
15 • 50   19 • 90
16 • 60

5 PAIR WORK Take turns saying a number from the chart. Your partner circles the number.

23	45	40	18	94	21	20	14
58	102	43	89	90	44	53	13
30	19	60	99	22	50	52	100
15	47	33	54	17	66	77	70
64	78	95	80	87	101	1	31

6 GRAMMAR • *Be*: questions with *How old*

How old is	he?	He's nineteen years old.
	she?	She's thirty-three.
	your sister?	She's twenty.

| How old are | they? | They're twenty-nine. |
| | your parents? | They're fifty and fifty-two. |

How old are you?
I'm three.

7 GRAMMAR PRACTICE Complete the questions. Use *How old is* or *How old are*.

1 .... your sister?
2 .... Matt's parents?
3 .... your grandfather?
4 .... Helen's husband?
5 .... her children?
6 .... his son?

NOW YOU CAN Talk about your family

1 CONVERSATION MODEL Read and listen.

A: I have one brother and two sisters.
B: Really? How old is your brother?
A: Twenty.
B: And your sisters?
A: Eighteen and twenty-two.

2 RHYTHM AND INTONATION Listen again and repeat. Then practice the Conversation Model with a partner.

3 PAIR WORK Personalize the conversation. Talk about your own family. Then change roles.

A: I have ....
B: Really? How old .... ?
A: ....
B: And your .... ?
A: ....

> **Don't stop!** Ask more questions.
> Tell me about your [mother].
> And your [father]?
> How about your [grandparents]?
> What's his / her name?
> What are their names?
> What's his / her occupation?
> What are their occupations?

4 CHANGE PARTNERS
Personalize the conversation again.

Extension

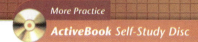

grammar • vocabulary • listening
reading • speaking • pronunciation

1 READING Read about some famous actors and their families and friends.

Who Are They?

This is **Jackie Chan**. Mr. Chan is an actor and a singer from Hong Kong. His wife is Joan Lin. She is an actress from Taiwan. Her Chinese name is Lin Feng-Jiao. They have a son, JC Chan. He's an actor and a singer, too.

This is **Abigail Breslin**. She's an actress from the United States. She's very young, and she's a movie star, too. She has two brothers, Ryan and Spencer. Spencer is also an actor. Miss Breslin lives with her parents, Michael and Kim Breslin, in New York. Her grandparents, Catherine and Lynn Blecker, say she's very cute in her movies.

This is **Gael García Bernal**, on the left, with his good friend, **Diego Luna**, on the right. Mr. García Bernal is a famous actor from Mexico. His parents, Patricia Bernal and José Ángel García, are actors, too. He has one sister and two brothers. Mr. Luna is also an actor. Many people think they are both very handsome.

2 READING COMPREHENSION Read about the people again. Complete the sentences.

1. Jackie Chan is JC Chan's ....
2. .... is Lin Feng-Jiao's husband.
3. Abigail Breslin's .... is an actor.
4. Miss Breslin is Lynn Blecker's ....
5. Gael García Bernal is Diego Luna's ....
6. Patricia Bernal, José Ángel García, and Diego Luna are ....

On your *ActiveBook* Self-Study Disc:
Extra Reading Comprehension Questions

3 PAIR WORK Interview your partner. Complete the notepad with information about your partner's family.

Relative's name	Relationship	Age	Occupation	Description
Doug	brother	14	student	He's very tall.

Relative's name	Relationship	Age	Occupation	Description

GRAMMAR BOOSTER
Extra practice • p. 138

4 GROUP WORK Now tell your classmates about your partner's family.

"Doug is Laura's brother. He's 14...."

"Tell Me All About It" Lyrics p. 147

Review

PAIR WORK

1 Ask and answer questions about the people. For example:
   A: Who's Meg?
   B: She's Sue's mother.
   A: Is Dora Meg's daughter?
   B: No, she's not.

2 Take turns making statements about the family relationships. For example:
   Mike has two children. Pia is his daughter.

DESCRIPTION Choose a photo. Use adjectives to describe the people in the family. For example:
   Pia is very cute.

WRITING Write ten sentences to describe the people in <u>your</u> family. For example:
   My grandparents are very good-looking.

NOW I CAN...
- ☐ Identify people in my family.
- ☐ Describe my relatives.
- ☐ Talk about my family.

UNIT 5

Events and Times

GOALS After Unit 5, you will be able to:
1. Confirm that you're on time.
2. Talk about the time of an event.
3. Ask about birthdays.

LESSON 1

GOAL Confirm that you're on time

1 🔊 **VOCABULARY** • *What time is it?* Read and listen. Then listen again and repeat.

1 It's one o'clock.
2 It's one fifteen. It's a quarter after one.
3 It's one twenty. It's twenty after one.
4 It's one thirty. It's half past one.

5 It's one forty. It's twenty to two.
6 It's one forty-five. It's a quarter to two.
7 It's noon.
8 It's midnight.

24:00 → 11:59 = A.M.
12:00 → 23:59 = P.M.

Say "eight A.M." or "eight P.M."

2 🔊 **PRONUNCIATION** • *Sentence rhythm* Read and listen. Then listen again and repeat.

  1 It's **TEN** after **FIVE**.   **2** It's **TWEN**ty to **ONE**.   **3** It's a **QUAR**ter to **TWO**.

3 PRONUNCIATION PRACTICE Read the times in the Vocabulary aloud again. Pay attention to sentence rhythm.

4 PAIR WORK Look at the map. Ask your partner about times around the world. Say each time two ways.

❝ What time is it in Vancouver? ❞

❝ It's nine forty A.M. It's twenty to ten. ❞

36   UNIT 5

5 🔊 **VOCABULARY** • *Early*, *on time*, and *late* Read and listen. Then listen again and repeat.

1 She's **early**.

2 They're **on time**.

3 He's **late**.

NOW YOU CAN Confirm that you're on time

1 🔊 **CONVERSATION MODEL** Read and listen.

   A: What time is the meeting?
   B: 10:00.
   A: Uh-oh. Am I late?
   B: No, you're not. It's five to ten.
   A: Five to ten?
   B: That's right. You're early.

2 🔊 **RHYTHM AND INTONATION** Listen again and repeat. Then practice the Conversation Model with a partner.

3 **PAIR WORK** It's 2:15 P.M. now. Change the model. Use the pictures. Then change roles.

   A: What time is the ....?
   B: ....
   A: Uh-oh. Am I late?
   B: .... It's ....
   A: ....?
   B: That's right. You're ....

class: 2:15 P.M.   train: 2:30 P.M.   bus: 2:00 P.M.

4 **CHANGE PARTNERS** Change the model again.

LESSON 2

GOAL Talk about the time of an event

VOCABULARY BOOSTER
More events • p. 128

1 🔊 **VOCABULARY** • *Events* Read and listen. Then listen again and repeat.

1 a party

2 a game

3 a dinner

4 a movie

5 a concert

2 🔊 **LISTENING COMPREHENSION** Listen to the conversations about events. Write the event and circle the time.

1 .... (7:15 / 7:45)
2 .... (8:00 / 9:00)
3 .... (3:30 / 3:15)
4 .... (12:00 A.M. / 12:00 P.M.)
5 .... (9:15 / 9:50)
6 .... (12:00 A.M. / 12:00 P.M.)

3 🔊 **VOCABULARY** • *Days of the week* Read and listen. Then listen again and repeat.

WEEKDAYS					THE WEEKEND	
Monday	Tuesday	Wednesday	Thursday	Friday	Saturday	Sunday

4 **GRAMMAR** • *Be:* questions about time / Prepositions <u>at</u> and <u>on</u>

What time is it? (It's) five twenty.
What time's the party? (It's) **at** nine thirty.
What day is the concert? (It's) **on** Saturday.
When's the dance? { (It's) **at** ten o'clock.
                        (It's) **on** Friday **at** 10:00 P.M.

Contractions
What time is → What time's
When is → When's

Be careful!
What time is it? NOT What ~~time's~~ it?
When is it? NOT ~~When's~~ it?

5 **GRAMMAR PRACTICE** Complete the questions and answers.

1. A: When .... the party?
   B: It's .... 11:00 P.M.
2. A: .... day is the game?
   B: It's .... Saturday.
3. A: What .... is the concert?
   B: It's .... 8:30.
4. A: What .... is the dinner?
   B: It's .... Tuesday.
5. A: .... is the film?
   B: It's .... Friday at 9:00.
6. A: What .... is the class?
   B: It's .... noon.

6 **LISTENING COMPREHENSION** Listen to the conversation. Write the events on the calendar.

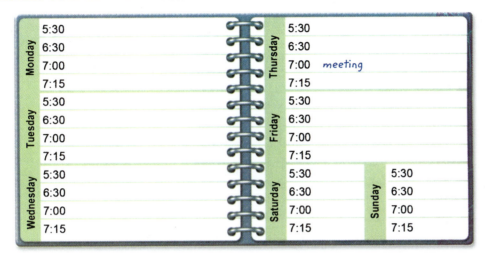

NOW YOU CAN   Talk about the time of an event

1. **CONVERSATION MODEL** Read and listen.

   A: Look. There's a play on Wednesday.
   B: Great! What time?
   A: 10:30. At Pat's theater.
   B: Really? Let's meet at 10:15.

2. **RHYTHM AND INTONATION** Listen again and repeat. Then practice the Conversation Model with a partner.

3. **PAIR WORK** Change the model. Ask your partner about an event. Use these events or your own events. Then change roles.

   A: Look. There's a .... on ....
   B: Great! What time?
   A: .... At ....
   B: Really? Let's meet at ....

4. **CHANGE PARTNERS** Talk about different events.

LESSON 3

GOAL Ask about birthdays

1 **VOCABULARY** • *Ordinal numbers* Read and listen. Then listen again and repeat.

1st first	2nd second	3rd third	4th fourth	5th fifth
6th sixth	7th seventh	8th eighth	9th ninth	10th tenth
11th eleventh	12th twelfth	13th thirteenth	14th fourteenth	15th fifteenth
16th sixteenth	17th seventeenth	18th eighteenth	19th nineteenth	20th twentieth
21st twenty-first	22nd twenty-second	30th thirtieth	40th fortieth	50th fiftieth

2 **PAIR WORK** Say a number. Your partner says the ordinal number.

"three"
"third"

3 **VOCABULARY** • *Months of the year* Read and listen. Then listen again and repeat.

January	February	March	April	May	June
S M T W T F S	S M T W T F S	S M T W T F S	S M T W T F S	S M T W T F S	S M T W T F S
1 2 3 4	1	1	1 2 3 4 5	1 2 3	1 2 3 4 5 6 7
5 6 7 8 9 10 11	2 3 4 5 6 7 8	2 3 4 5 6 7 8	6 7 8 9 10 11 12	4 5 6 7 8 9 10	8 9 10 11 12 13 14
12 13 14 15 16 17 18	9 10 11 12 13 14 15	9 10 11 12 13 14 15	13 14 15 16 17 18 19	11 12 13 14 15 16 17	15 16 17 18 19 20 21
19 20 21 22 23 24 25	16 17 18 19 20 21 22	16 17 18 19 20 21 22	20 21 22 23 24 25 26	18 19 20 21 22 23 24	22 23 24 25 26 27 28
26 27 28 29 30 31	23 24 25 26 27 28	23 24 25 26 27 28 29 30 31	27 28 29 30	25 26 27 28 29 30 31	29 30

July	August	September	October	November	December
S M T W T F S	S M T W T F S	S M T W T F S	S M T W T F S	S M T W T F S	S M T W T F S
1 2 3 4 5	1 2	1 2 3 4 5 6	1 2 3 4	1	1 2 3 4 5 6
6 7 8 9 10 11 12	3 4 5 6 7 8 9	7 8 9 10 11 12 13	5 6 7 8 9 10 11	2 3 4 5 6 7 8	7 8 9 10 11 12 13
13 14 15 16 17 18 19	10 11 12 13 14 15 16	14 15 16 17 18 19 20	12 13 14 15 16 17 18	9 10 11 12 13 14 15	14 15 16 17 18 19 20
20 21 22 23 24 25 26	17 18 19 20 21 22 23	21 22 23 24 25 26 27	19 20 21 22 23 24 25	16 17 18 19 20 21 22	21 22 23 24 25 26 27
27 28 29 30 31	24 25 26 27 28 29 30 31	28 29 30	26 27 28 29 30 31	23 24 25 26 27 28 29 30	28 29 30 31

4 **LISTENING COMPREHENSION** Listen to the dates. Circle the dates on the calendar.

5 **PAIR WORK** Say a date from the calendar. Your partner writes the date.

"July thirty-first" July 31st

40 UNIT 5

6 GRAMMAR • Prepositions <u>in</u>, <u>on</u>, and <u>at</u> for dates and times: summary

When's the party?	**In** January.
When's the meeting?	**On** Tuesday.
When's the play?	**On** January 15th.
When's the dinner?	**On** the 12th.
What time's the movie?	**At** noon.
What time's the play?	**At** 8:30.

Be careful!
in the morning
in the afternoon
in the evening
BUT **at** night

7 GRAMMAR PRACTICE Complete the sentences. Use <u>in</u>, <u>on</u>, or <u>at</u>.

1 The concert is .... July 14th .... 3:00 .... the afternoon.
2 The dinner is .... December .... the 6th.
3 The party is .... midnight .... Saturday.
4 The movie is .... November 1st .... 8:30 P.M.
5 The game is .... Wednesday .... noon.
6 The meeting is at the State Bank .... 11:00 .... the morning .... July 18th.

NOW YOU CAN Ask about birthdays

1 2:31 **CONVERSATION MODEL** Read and listen.

A: When's your birthday?
B: On July 15th. When's yours?
A: My birthday's in November. On the 13th.

2 2:32 **RHYTHM AND INTONATION** Listen again and repeat. Then practice the Conversation Model with a partner.

3 PAIR WORK Personalize the conversation with your own birthdays.

A: When's your birthday?
B: .... When's yours?
A: My birthday's ....

Don't stop!
Ask questions to complete the chart.

brother's birthday:
sister's birthday:
mother's birthday:
father's birthday:
grandmother's birthday:
grandfather's birthday:

4 CHANGE PARTNERS Ask about other people's birthdays.

2:33 On someone's birthday say:

" Happy birthday! "   " Thank you! "

Extension

More Practice
ActiveBook Self-Study Disc

grammar · vocabulary · listening
reading · speaking · pronunciation

1 🔊 **READING** Read the conversations. What are the events?

1 A: Hey, it's Alec's birthday on June 1st.
B: Really? That's on Friday.
A: That's right. And there's a party.
B: Great! Where?
A: At the New School, right around the corner.
B: What time?
A: 11:30.

2 A: There's a game tomorrow at 10:30.
B: Hey, let's go! Where is it?
A: At Casey's Restaurant.
B: Is that next to the bookstore?
A: That's right.

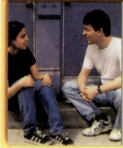

3 A: There's a movie tonight at 8:00.
B: Really? What movie?
A: The Party, with Peter Sellers.
B: The English actor?
A: Right.
B: That's an old movie!
A: Yes, but it's good. Let's go. OK?

4 A: Where is the meeting?
B: At United Bank.
A: Can we walk there?
B: No, let's go by taxi.
A: Are we late?
B: No. The meeting's at 10:00. It's only 9:30.

2 INTEGRATED PRACTICE Correct all the mistakes. Use the information in the Reading.

1 The game is at half past ~~nine~~ ten.
2 The movie is at 8:00 A.M.
3 The meeting is at half past ten.
4 The birthday party is at midnight.
5 Alec's birthday is in July.
6 The meeting is at the bookstore.
7 The meeting is at the New School.
8 Alec's party is at United Bank.
9 United Bank is around the corner.
10 Peter Sellers is an English singer.

On your *ActiveBook* Self-Study Disc:
Extra Reading Comprehension Questions

GRAMMAR BOOSTER
Extra practice • p. 139

Top Notch Pop
"Let's Make a Date" Lyrics p. 147

42   UNIT 5

Review

PAIR WORK Create conversations for the people.
1 Talk about the events. For example:
   Look. There's a ___ ...
2 Confirm that you are on time for an event. For example:
   What time's the ___ ?

CONTEST Study the events for one minute. Then close your books. Who can remember all the times, dates, and locations? For example:
   There's a ___ on ___ at ___ .

WRITING Write five sentences about events at your school or in your city. For example:
   There's a concert on Friday at ...

NOW I CAN... ✓
- ☐ Confirm that I'm on time.
- ☐ Talk about the time of an event.
- ☐ Ask about birthdays.

UNIT 6

Clothes

GOALS After Unit 6, you will be able to:
1 Give and accept a compliment.
2 Ask for colors and sizes.
3 Describe clothes.

LESSON 1

GOAL Give and accept a compliment

VOCABULARY BOOSTER
More clothes • p. 129

1 🔊 2:37 **VOCABULARY** • *Clothes* Read and listen. Then listen again and repeat.

1 a shirt   2 a sweater   3 a tie   4 a jacket   5 a skirt   6 shoes   7 a dress   8 a suit   9 a blouse   10 pants*

* Pants is a plural noun. Use <u>are</u>, not <u>is</u>, with <u>pants</u>.

2 🔊 2:38 **PRONUNCIATION** • *Plurals* Read and listen. Then listen again and repeat.

1 /s/ shirts = shirt/s/   2 /z/ shoes = shoe/z/   3 /ɪz/ blouses = blouse/ɪz/
jackets = jacket/s/   sweaters = sweater/z/   dresses = dress/ɪz/

3 GRAMMAR • *Demonstratives* <u>this</u>, <u>that</u>, <u>these</u>, <u>those</u>

this sweater   that sweater   these ties   those ties

4 GRAMMAR PRACTICE Look at the pictures. Write <u>this</u>, <u>that</u>, <u>these</u>, or <u>those</u> and the name of the clothes.

1 *those jackets*   2 ....   3 ....   4 ....

5 .... 6 .... 7 .... 8 ....

5 GRAMMAR • The simple present tense: affirmative statements with like, want, need, and have

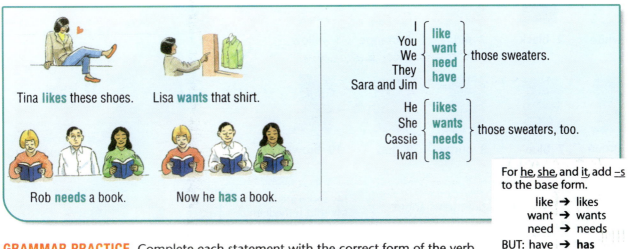

6 GRAMMAR PRACTICE Complete each statement with the correct form of the verb.

1 I .... your tie.
    like / likes
2 My friends .... this suit.
    want / wants
3 Janet .... this skirt.
    need / needs
4 Peter .... that jacket.
    have / has
5 We .... our dresses.
    like / likes
6 Sue and Tara .... those suits.
    want / wants

NOW YOU CAN Give and accept a compliment

1 🔊 **CONVERSATION MODEL** Read and listen.
   2:39

  A: I like that dress.
  B: Thank you.
  A: You're welcome.

2 🔊 **RHYTHM AND INTONATION** Listen again and repeat.
   2:40
Then practice the Conversation Model with a partner.

3 **PAIR WORK** Personalize the conversation. Compliment your classmates on their clothes and shoes. Then change roles.

  A: I like ....
  B: ....
  A: You're welcome.

4 **CHANGE PARTNERS** Compliment other classmates' clothes.

LESSON 2

GOAL Ask for colors and sizes

1 **VOCABULARY** • *Colors and sizes* Read and listen. Then listen again and repeat.

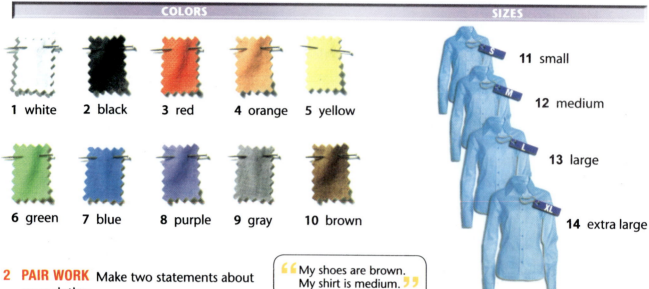

2 **PAIR WORK** Make two statements about your clothes.

 "My shoes are brown. My shirt is medium."

3 **GRAMMAR** • *The simple present tense: negative statements and yes / no questions with* like, want, need, *and* have

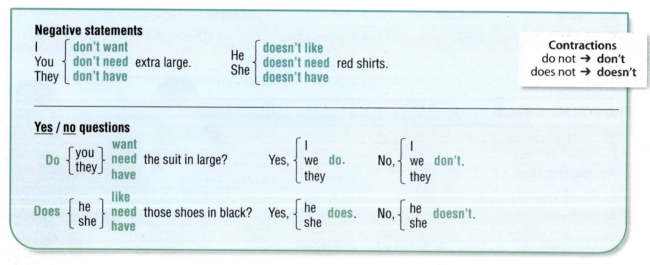

4 **GRAMMAR PRACTICE** Complete the sentences with the correct form of the verb. Use contractions.

1 A: ...Do... your children ...have... sweaters for school?
   B: My daughter ...does..., but my son ...doesn't... .

2 A: .... your husband .... a black tie? (need)
   B: No, he .... He .... two black ties. (have)

3 A: I .... a blue suit for work. .... you (need) .... one too? (need)
   B: Yes, I ....

4 A: .... you .... that green shirt? (like)
   B: Actually, no, I ....

5 A: We .... the clothes in this store. (not like)
   B: Really, that's too bad. We ....

6 A: .... you .... this black jacket in size 34? (have)
   B: No, I'm sorry. We ....

5 🔊 **LISTENING COMPREHENSION** Listen to the conversations about clothes. For each statement, circle T (true) or F (false). Then listen again and circle the color.

T F **1** They like the dress.   T F **4** He needs a tie.

T F **2** He needs shoes.   T F **5** She needs the sweater in small.

T F **3** Matt needs a suit for work.    T F **6** They don't have his size.

NOW YOU CAN Ask for colors and sizes

1 🔊 **CONVERSATION MODEL** Read and listen.

A: Do you have this sweater in green?

B: Yes, we do.

A: Great. And my husband needs a shirt. Do you have that shirt in large?

B: No, I'm sorry. We don't.

A: That's too bad.

2 🔊 **RHYTHM AND INTONATION** Listen again and repeat. Then practice the Conversation Model with a partner.

3 **PAIR WORK** Now change the model. Ask for colors and sizes of clothes for you and a member of your family. Use the pictures. Then change roles.

A: Do you have .... in .... ?

B: ....

A: .... And my .... needs .... Do you have .... in .... ?

B: ....

A: ....

4 **CHANGE PARTNERS** Practice the conversation again. Ask about other clothes.

LESSON 3

GOAL Describe clothes

1 🔊 **VOCABULARY** • *Opposite adjectives to describe clothes* Read and listen. Then listen again and repeat.

1 new   2 old   3 dirty   4 clean
5 loose   6 tight   7 cheap   8 expensive   9 long   10 short

2 **GRAMMAR** • *Adjective placement*

> **Adjectives come before the nouns they describe.**
>   a **long** skirt   **tight** shoes   a **red** and **black** tie
>
> **Adjectives don't change.**
>   a **clean** shirt / **clean** shirts   NOT ~~cleans~~ shirts.
>
> **Be careful!**
>   It's a **long skirt**.   NOT   It's a ~~skirt long~~.

3 **PAIR WORK** Look at your classmates. Take turns describing their clothes.

> ❝ Allen has new shoes. ❞
>
> ❝ Joe's shoes are old.
>   He needs new shoes. ❞

4 **GRAMMAR PRACTICE** Write two descriptions for each picture. Follow the model.

1 The <u>blouses</u> are <u>clean</u>.
   They're <u>clean blouses</u>.

2 The .... is ....
   It's ....

3 The .... are ....
   They're ....

48   UNIT 6

5 GRAMMAR • *The simple present tense: questions with What, Why, and Which / One and ones*

Use a question word and do or does to ask information questions in the simple present tense.
What do you need? (A blue and white tie.)   What does she want? (New shoes.)

Use because to answer questions with Why.
Why do they want that suit? (Because it's nice.)   Why does he like this tie? (Because it's green.)

Use Which to ask about choice. Answer with one or ones.
Which sweater do you want? (The blue one.)   Which shoes does she like? (The black ones.)

6 GRAMMAR PRACTICE
Complete the conversations. Answer each question in your own words. Then practice the conversations with a partner.

1. A: Which skirt .... ? (she / want)
   B: The .... one.

2. A: What .... ? (your friend / need)
   B: ....

3. A: What color shoes .... ? (you / like)
   B: ....

4. A: Why .... new shoes? (you / want)
   B: ....

5. A: Which shirts .... ? (you / like)
   B: The .... ones.

6. A: What size shoes .... ? (you / need)
   B: ....

NOW YOU CAN Describe clothes

1 CONVERSATION MODEL Read and listen. 2:46

A: What do you think of this jacket?
B: I think it's nice. What about you?
A: Well, it's nice, but it's a little tight.
B: Let's keep looking.

2 RHYTHM AND INTONATION Listen again and repeat. Then practice the Conversation Model with a partner. 2:47

3 PAIR WORK Now change the model. Use different clothes. Use different problems. Then change roles.

A: What do you think of .... ?
B: I think .... nice. What about you?
A: Well, ... nice, but .... a little ....
B: Let's keep looking.

♻ **Be sure to recycle this language.**

Clothes		Problems
shirt	pants	expensive
sweater	skirt	tight
dress	jacket	loose
tie	shoes	long
		short

4 CHANGE PARTNERS Talk about different clothes and problems.

Extension

More Practice
ActiveBook Self-Study Disc

grammar · vocabulary · listening
reading · speaking · pronunciation

1 🔊 **READING** Read the advertisement from today's newspaper. Which clothes do you like?

2:48

TODAY ONLY!
1/2 Price Sale

THE EMPORIUM
A Great Clothes Store!

Low, Low Prices!
MEN'S & WOMEN'S CLOTHES
ALL STORES OPEN UNTIL MIDNIGHT

Many more styles available.

Blue at King Street store only.

White not available at South Street Station location.

Other sale items today: Children's jackets and shoes
STORE LOCATIONS: 62 KING STREET, THE UPTOWN MALL, AND SOUTH STREET STATION.

2 READING COMPREHENSION Read the statements about the advertisement. Check <u>True</u> or <u>False</u>.

	True	False			True	False
1 The sale is every day this week.	☐	☐	5 All locations have blue sweaters.	☐	☐
2 The store has three locations.	☐	☐	6 The Emporium doesn't have children's shoes.	☐	☐
3 The Emporium is a clothes store.	☐	☐			
4 White blouses are on sale at two locations.	☐	☐			

On your *ActiveBook* Self-Study Disc:
Extra Reading Comprehension Questions

3 PAIR WORK Discuss the sale at the Emporium. Use the advertisement.

♻ **Be sure to recycle this language.**

Do you want ___ ?
Do you like this / that ___ ?
Do you need [a gray] ___ ?
What do you need / like / want / have?
Which ___ do you ___ ?
Why do you ___ these / those ___ ?

"What do you need?"

"I need a white blouse for work, and my children need shoes for school. Let's go to the Emporium. They have a great sale."

GRAMMAR BOOSTER
Extra practice • p. 140

50   UNIT 6

Review

GAME Describe people's clothes. Your partner points to the picture. For example:
He has a yellow shirt.

PAIR WORK

1 Point and ask and answer questions about the picture. Use <u>this</u> / <u>that</u> / <u>these</u> / <u>those</u> and <u>like</u>, <u>want</u>, <u>need</u>, and <u>have</u>. For example:
Do you like these shoes?

2 Create conversations for the people. For example:
A: *Do you want these pants?*
B: *No, I don't.*

WRITING Write about clothes you need, you want, you like, and clothes you have or don't have. For example:
I need a new white blouse. My old blouse is a little tight. I want red shoes and a long skirt...

NOW I CAN...
☐ Give and accept a compliment.
☐ Ask for colors and sizes.
☐ Describe clothes.

UNIT 7

Activities

GOALS After Unit 7, you will be able to:
1. Talk about morning and evening activities.
2. Describe what you do in your free time.
3. Discuss household chores.

LESSON 1

GOAL Talk about morning and evening activities

1 **VOCABULARY** • *Daily activities at home* Read and listen. Then listen again and repeat.

1 get up   2 get dressed   3 brush my teeth   4 comb / brush my hair   5 shave

6 eat breakfast   7 come home   8 make dinner   9 study   10 watch TV

11 get undressed   12 take a shower / a bath   13 go to bed

2 **PAIR WORK** Tell your partner about your daily activities.

"I eat lunch at 12:00."

Meals
breakfast
lunch
dinner

3 **GRAMMAR** • *The simple present tense: spelling rules with* he, she, *and* it

Add **–s** to the base form of most verbs
 get**s**   shave**s**   comb**s**

Add **–es** to verbs that end in **–s**, **–sh**, **–ch**, or **–x**.
 brush**es**   watch**es**

Remember:
do → does
go → goes
have → has
study → studies

4 GRAMMAR PRACTICE Complete the statements. Use the simple present tense.

1. Tom .... (get) up at 6:00, but his wife, Kate, ... (get) up at 7:00.
2. Kate .... (eat) breakfast at 7:30 A.M., but Tom .... (eat) breakfast at 6:30.
3. After breakfast, Tom .... (shave), and Kate .... (put) on makeup.
4. Tom and Kate .... (watch) TV in the evening.
5. Kate .... (go) to bed at 10:00 P.M., but Tom .... (go) to bed at 11:00.
6. Kate .... (make) dinner on weekdays, and Tom .... (make) dinner on weekends.
7. Tom .... (take) a shower in the morning, but Kate .... (take) a bath.
8. Tom and Kate .... (brush) their teeth in the morning and in the evening.

5 GRAMMAR • The simple present tense: questions with *When* and *What time*

When **do** you **take** a shower? (In the morning.)
What time **does** she **get** up? (Before 7:00 A.M.)

before 8:00   7:45 | after 8:00   8:15

6 GRAMMAR PRACTICE
On a separate sheet of paper, write five questions about Tom and Kate in Exercise 4. Then listen to and answer a classmate's questions aloud.

1. What time does Kate get up?
  "She gets up at 7:00."

NOW YOU CAN Talk about morning and evening activities

3:04
1. CONVERSATION MODEL Read and listen.
   A: Are you a morning person or an evening person?
   B: Me? I'm definitely an evening person.
   A: And why do you say that?
   B: Well, I get up after ten in the morning. And I go to bed after two. What about you?
   A: I'm a morning person. I get up before six.

3:05
2. RHYTHM AND INTONATION Listen again and repeat. Then practice the Conversation Model with a partner.

3. PAIR WORK Personalize the conversation. Use your own information.
   A: Are you a morning person or an evening person?
   B: Me? I'm definitely ....
   A: And why do you say that?
   B: Well, I .... What about you?
   A: I'm .... I ....

4. CHANGE PARTNERS Personalize the conversation again.

5. CLASS SURVEY Find out how many students are morning people and how many are evening people.

Don't stop! Ask more questions.

♻ Be sure to recycle this language.
When do you ___ ?
What time do you ___ ?
What about your [parents]?

LESSON 2

GOAL Describe what you do in your free time

1 🔊 **VOCABULARY** • *Leisure activities* Read and listen. Then listen again and repeat.

1 exercise

2 take a nap

3 listen to music

4 read

5 play soccer

6 check e-mail

7 go out for dinner

8 go to the movies

9 visit friends

2 **INTEGRATED PRACTICE** Write six questions for a classmate about his or her leisure activities. Use <u>When</u> or <u>What time</u> and the simple present tense.

1 *When do you visit friends?*

1	4
2	5
3	6

3 **GRAMMAR** • *The simple present tense: frequency adverbs*

100% ↑ I **always** play soccer on Saturday.
       I **usually** check e-mail in the evening.
       I **sometimes** go dancing on weekends.
0% ↓ I **never** take a nap in the afternoon.

Be careful!
Place the frequency adverb before the verb in the simple present tense.
Don't say: I ~~play always~~ soccer.
             He ~~checks usually~~ e-mail.

4 **PAIR WORK** Now use your questions from Exercise 2 to ask your partner about leisure activities. Use frequency adverbs and time expressions in your answers.

"When do you visit friends?"

"I usually visit friends on Saturday."

5 GRAMMAR PRACTICE Write sentences about your partner from Exercise 4 on a separate sheet of paper.

> Scott usually visits friends on Saturday.

NOW YOU CAN Describe what you do in your free time

1 🔊 CONVERSATION MODEL Read and listen.
3:07

A: What's your typical day like?
B: Well, I usually go to work at 9:00 and come home at 6:00.
A: And what do you do in your free time?
B: I sometimes read or watch TV. What about you?
A: Pretty much the same.

2 🔊 RHYTHM AND INTONATION Listen again and repeat. Then practice the Conversation Model with a partner.
3:08

3 PAIR WORK Write your typical daily activities on the notepad. Then personalize the conversation with your own information.

A: What's your typical day like?
B: Well, I ....
A: And what do you do in your free time?
B: .... What about you?
A: ....

Don't stop!
Ask about other times and days.

♻ Be sure to recycle this language.

Time expressions
in the morning	at night
in the afternoon	on [Friday]
in the evening	

4 CHANGE PARTNERS Personalize the conversation again.

5 GROUP WORK Tell the class about your partner's activities.

On weekdays

On weekends

LESSON 3

GOAL Discuss household chores

VOCABULARY BOOSTER
More household chores • p. 129

1 🔊 **VOCABULARY** • *Household chores* Read and listen. Then listen again and repeat.

1 wash the dishes

2 clean the house

3 do the laundry

4 take out the garbage

5 go shopping

2 **GRAMMAR** • *The simple present tense: questions with* How often / *Other time expressions*

	M	T	W	T	F	S	S
How often **do** you **take** out the garbage? I take out the garbage **every day**.	✓	✓	✓	✓	✓	✓	✓

	M	T	W	T	F	S	S
How often **does** she **go** shopping? She goes shopping **on Saturdays**.						✓	
						✓	

Other time expressions	M	T	W	T	F	S	S
once a week	✓						
twice a week		✓		✓			
three times a week		✓		✓	✓		

Also
- once a year
- twice a day
- three times a month
- every weekend
- every Friday

3 **PAIR WORK** Ask and answer questions about how often you do household chores.

"How often do you go shopping?"
"Twice a week."

4 🔊 **PRONUNCIATION** • *Third-person singular verb endings* Read and listen. Then listen again and repeat.

1 /s/	2 /z/	3 /ɪz/
takes = take /s/	cleans = clean /z/	washes = wash /ɪz/
checks = check /s/	does = doe /z/	practices = practice /ɪz/
makes = make /s/	plays = play /z/	exercises = exercise /ɪz/

5 **INTEGRATED PRACTICE** Tell your class how often your partner from Exercise 3 does household chores. Practice pronunciation of third-person verb endings.

"John **goes** shopping twice a week."

6 **GRAMMAR** • *The simple present tense: questions with* Who *as subject*

Who washes the dishes in your family? { I do. / My sister does.
                                             We do. / My grandparents do.

Be careful!
Always use a third-person singular verb when **who** is the subject.
   Don't say: Who ~~clean~~ the house?
Don't use **do** or **does** when **who** is the subject.
   Don't say: Who ~~does clean~~ the house?

UNIT 7

7 **LISTENING COMPREHENSION** Listen to the conversations and the questions with <u>Who</u>. Check the chores each person does.

1	She…	○	○	○	○	○
	Her husband…	○	○	○	○	○
	Her son…	○	○	○	○	○
	Her daughter…	○	○	○	○	○
2	He…	○	○	○	○	○
	His brother…	○	○	○	○	○
	His sister…	○	○	○	○	○
3	She…	○	○	○	○	○
	Her husband…	○	○	○	○	○
4	He…	○	○	○	○	○
	His wife…	○	○	○	○	○
	His son…	○	○	○	○	○

8 **GRAMMAR PRACTICE** With a partner, ask and answer questions about the people in Exercise 7.

" In Conversation 1, who washes the dishes? "
" Her husband does. "

NOW YOU CAN Discuss household chores

1 **CONVERSATION MODEL** Read and listen.

A: So how often do you do the laundry?
B: About twice a week. How about you?
A: Me? I never do the laundry. Could I ask another question?
B: Sure.
A: Who cleans the house?
B: Oh, that's my brother's job.

2 **RHYTHM AND INTONATION** Listen again and repeat. Then practice the Conversation Model with a partner. Then change roles.

3 **PAIR WORK** Personalize the conversation.

A: So how often do you ………?
B: ……… . How about you?
A: Me? ……… . Could I ask another question?
B: ……… .
A: Who ………?
B: Oh, that's ……… 's job.

Don't stop!
Ask about other chores.

4 **CHANGE PARTNERS** Ask another classmate about household chores.

5 **GROUP WORK** Tell your classmates about your partner's household chores.

Extension

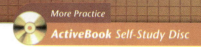

More Practice
ActiveBook Self-Study Disc

grammar • vocabulary • listening
reading • speaking • pronunciation

1 🔊 3:14 **READING** Read the article. Do you like housework?

Don't like household chores?
These robots help!

How often do you clean your house? Once a week? Twice a month? Never? Well, these two robots clean the house for you. The iRobot Roomba turns right or left, and vacuums while you watch TV or exercise. Take a nap, and the house is clean when you get up. And if you want to wash the floor, the iRobot Scooba washes the floor for you. The Scooba moves around corners and washes the floor while you listen to music or check your e-mail. Now that's help with household chores!

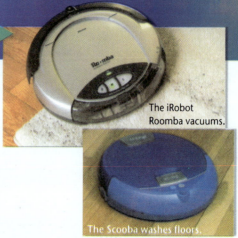

The iRobot Roomba vacuums.

The Scooba washes floors.

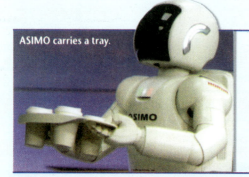

ASIMO carries a tray.

And who is this? Meet ASIMO, a robot from the Honda Motor Company. ASIMO doesn't clean the house. It doesn't wash dishes or take out the garbage. But ASIMO walks and carries things. Say "turn left" or "turn right," and ASIMO turns.

No one wants to mow the lawn. But the L200 Evolution lawn mower mows the lawn for you. Tell the robot what time you want to mow. How about midnight, after you go to bed? It mows the lawn while you sleep. How about in the afternoon? It mows the lawn while you go out for lunch or go shopping.

The L200 mows lawns.

Sources: www.irobot.com, world.honda.com/ASIMO, www.robotlawnmowers.ie

On your *ActiveBook* Self-Study Disc:
Extra Reading Comprehension Questions

2 **READING COMPREHENSION** Complete each statement. Circle the correct verb.

1 The Roomba (washes / **vacuums** / mows).
2 The Scooba (**washes** / vacuums / mows).
3 The Roomba and the Scooba (wash / **clean** / vacuum).
4 The L200 Evolution (washes / **mows** / cleans).
5 ASIMO (washes / mows / **walks**).

3 **INTEGRATED PRACTICE** On a separate sheet of paper, write five sentences about the robots. Use the simple present tense.

4 **DISCUSSION** Which robots do you like? Do you want any of them? Why?

❝ I want the Roomba because it cleans the house. ❞

GRAMMAR BOOSTER
Extra practice • p. 140

🎵 3:15–3:16
Top Notch Pop
"On the Weekend"   Lyrics p. 147

58   UNIT 7

Jack's Typical Day

Morning

7:00 A.M.

7:10 A.M.

7:45 A.M.

8:15 A.M.

8:30 A.M.

Evening

6:00 P.M.

6:30 P.M.

7:00 P.M.

7:30 P.M.

8:00 P.M.

10:15 P.M.

11:00 P.M.

Review

CONTEST Study the photos for one minute. Then close your books. Who remembers all Jack's activities?

PAIR WORK Create a conversation for Jack and a friend. Start like this:

Jack, are you a morning person or an evening person? OR: *What's your typical day like?*

TRUE OR FALSE? Make statements about Jack's activities. Your partner says True or False. Take turns. For example:

A: *Jack usually takes a shower in the evening.*
B: *False. He takes a shower in the morning.*

WRITING Describe your typical week. Use adverbs of frequency and time expressions. For example:

I exercise every weekend.

NOW I CAN...

☐ Talk about morning and evening activities.
☐ Describe what I do in my free time.
☐ Discuss household chores.

Units 1–7 Review

3:17

1 🔊 **LISTENING COMPREHENSION** Listen to the conversations. Check each statement T (<u>true</u>) or F (<u>false</u>). Then listen again and check your work.

T F
- ☐ ☐ 1 She's a manager.
- ☐ ☐ 2 He's a doctor.
- ☐ ☐ 3 She's an architect.

T F
- ☐ ☐ 4 He's a student.
- ☐ ☐ 5 They're artists.
- ☐ ☐ 6 She's his neighbor.

2 PAIR WORK Ask and answer questions about places on the maps.   "Where's ___?"   "It's ___."

3 GRAMMAR PRACTICE Complete each sentence with <u>in</u>, <u>on</u>, or <u>at</u>.

1 The movie is …… Friday …… 8:00.
2 The meeting is …… June 6th …… the morning.
3 The party is …… Saturday …… midnight.
4 The dinner is …… April.
5 The dance is …… 8:00 P.M. …… Friday.

4 GRAMMAR PRACTICE Complete the sentences with <u>this</u>, <u>that</u>, <u>these</u>, or <u>those</u>.

1 I want ………… pants.
2 I like ………… jackets.
3 I like ………… suit.
4 I want ………… tie.

5 PAIR WORK

Partner A: Ask these questions. Partner B: Read the correct response to each question aloud.

1 Does he have grandchildren?
 a Yes, he has two sons.
 b Yes, he does.
2 Where's the pharmacy?
 a Don't walk. Take the bus.
 b It's around the corner.
3 Are we late?
 a Yes, you're early.
 b Yes. It's 10:00.

Partner B: Ask these questions. Partner A: Read the correct response to each question aloud.

4 When's the dance?
 a On Saturday.
 b At the school.
5 Do you like this suit?
 a Yes, I do.
 b Yes, it is.
6 How do you go to work?
 a I walk.
 b Walk.

6 PAIR WORK Write your own response to each person. Then practice your conversations with a partner.

1. Hi. I'm John. YOU *Nice to meet you* .
2. What's your last name? YOU ....
3. Do you have children? YOU ....
4. What time is it? YOU ....
5. When's your birthday? YOU ....
6. What do you do? YOU ....

7 GRAMMAR PRACTICE Look at the pictures. Write an imperative for each.

1. ...*Walk*......... to the bank.   2. .... to work.   3. .... to the pharmacy.

4. .... to the restaurant.   5. .... to school.   6. .... to the bookstore.

8 CONVERSATION PRACTICE With a partner, exchange real information about your families. Start like this:

" Tell me about your family. "

Ideas
Ask about names.   Ask about occupations.
Ask about ages.   Describe people.

9 🔊 **LISTENING COMPREHENSION** Listen to the conversations. Answer the questions. Then listen again and check your work.

1 What's her phone number?	It's __ __ __ - __ __ __ - __ __ __ __ .
2 What's his last name?	It's __ __ __ __ __ __ .
3 How old is his son?	He's __ years old.
4 What's the address?	It's __ __ West 12th Street.
5 What time is it?	It's 2: __ __ .

10 GRAMMAR PRACTICE Circle the correct word or words to complete each statement or question.

1 Is he (your / you) husband?
2 Is she (their / they) granddaughter?
3 (Her / His) name is Mr. Grant.
4 (Our / We) birthdays are in May.
5 How do you spell (her / she) name?
6 I'm (Ms. Bell / Ms. Bell's) student.

11 INTEGRATED PRACTICE Write a question for each response.

1 A: ....?
   B: No. She's a student.
2 A: ....?
   B: I'm an architect.
3 A: ....?
   B: The bank is across the street.
4 A: ....?
   B: It's 9:45.
5 A: ....?
   B: It's 34 Bank Street.
6 A: ....?
   B: The newsstand is around the corner.
7 A: ....?
   B: My birthday? In February.
8 A: ....?
   B: They're my sisters.

12 PAIR WORK

Partner A: Ask these questions. Partner B: Read the correct response to each question aloud.

1 Does Jack have a large family?
   a Yes, I do.
   b Yes, he does.
2 Does her father shave every morning?
   a Yes, he is.
   b No, he doesn't.
3 Is Ms. Wang his English teacher?
   a Yes, he is.
   b Yes, she is.

Partner B: Ask these questions. Partner A: Read the correct response to each question aloud.

4 Does she like red shoes?
   a No, she doesn't.
   b Yes, I do.
5 Does he need a new tie?
   a Yes, he does.
   b Yes, I do.
6 Does she always clean the house on Sunday?
   a Yes, she is.
   b Yes, she does.

13 GRAMMAR PRACTICE Circle the correct verb to complete each sentence.

1 We (am / are) friends.
2 They (has / have) two children.
3 Who (has / have) a blue suit?
4 (Do / Does) she (want / wants) new shoes?
5 Why (do / does) they (need / needs) new shoes?
6 (Is / Are) we on time?

14 GRAMMAR PRACTICE Complete the statements with verbs in the simple present tense.

1 I usually .... TV in the evening, but my brother .... to music.
2 We sometimes .... the house and .... the laundry in the morning.
3 After dinner, I always .... the dishes and my wife .... out the garbage.
4 My neighbors never .... shopping on weekdays.
5 My sister always .... to bed before 10:00 P.M., but I usually .... e-mail at 10:00.
6 My grandfather always .... a nap in the afternoon.

15 INTEGRATED PRACTICE On a separate sheet of paper, answer the questions. Use frequency adverbs or time expressions. Then tell your classmates about your activities.

1 What do you do on weekends?
2 What do you do after breakfast?
3 What do you do after work or school?
4 What do you do at night before you go to bed?

> 1 I usually go shopping on weekends.

16 CONVERSATION PRACTICE With a partner, talk about the times of events. Use the pictures or your own ideas. Start like this:

❝ Look. There's a ___ on ___ . ❞

♺ **Be sure to recycle this language.**

Really?
What time?
Let's go!
Good idea.
across the street
down the street
around the corner

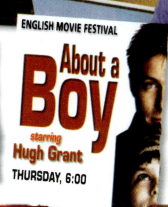

Other events
a meeting
a party
a dinner
your own idea ___

Reference Charts

Countries and nationalities

Country	Nationality	Country	Nationality	Country	Nationality
Argentina	Argentinean / Argentine	Guatemala	Guatemalan	Peru	Peruvian
Australia	Australian	Holland	Dutch	Poland	Polish
Belgium	Belgian	Honduras	Honduran	Portugal	Portuguese
Bolivia	Bolivian	Hungary	Hungarian	Russia	Russian
Brazil	Brazilian	India	Indian	Saudi Arabia	Saudi / Saudi Arabian
Canada	Canadian	Indonesia	Indonesian	Spain	Spanish
Chile	Chilean	Ireland	Irish	Sweden	Swedish
China	Chinese	Italy	Italian	Switzerland	Swiss
Colombia	Colombian	Japan	Japanese	Taiwan	Chinese
Costa Rica	Costa Rican	Korea	Korean	Thailand	Thai
Ecuador	Ecuadorian	Lebanon	Lebanese	Turkey	Turkish
Egypt	Egyptian	Malaysia	Malaysian	the United Kingdom	British
El Salvador	Salvadorean	Mexico	Mexican	the United States	American
France	French	Nicaragua	Nicaraguan	Uruguay	Uruguayan
Germany	German	Panama	Panamanian	Venezuela	Venezuelan
Greece	Greek	Paraguay	Paraguayan	Vietnam	Vietnamese

Numbers 100 to 1,000,000,000

100	one hundred	1,000	one thousand	10,000	ten thousand	1,000,000	one million
500	five hundred	5,000	five thousand	100,000	one hundred thousand	1,000,000,000	one billion

Irregular verbs

This is an alphabetical list of all irregular verbs in the *Top Notch Fundamentals* units. The page number refers to the page on which the base form of the verb first appears.

base form	simple past	page	base form	simple past	page	base form	simple past	page
be	was / were	4	get	got	52	say	said	90
break	broke	98	go	went	25	see	saw	85
buy	bought	76	grow	grew	112	sing	sang	104
can	could	23	hang out	hung out	114	sleep	slept	114
come	came	52	have	had	32	study	studied	52
cut	cut	98	hurt	hurt	98	swim	swam	104
do	did	52	lie	lay	100	take	took	22
draw	drew	104	make	made	52	teach	taught	84
drink	drank	85	meet	met	1	tell	told	88
drive	drove	22	put	put	52	think	thought	90
eat	ate	52	read	read	54	wear	wore	72
fall	fell	98	ride	rode	92	write	wrote	5
feel	felt	100						

Pronunciation table

These are the pronunciation symbols used in *Top Notch Fundamentals*.

Vowels

Symbol	Key Words	Symbol	Key Words
i	feed	ə	banana, around
ɪ	did	ɚ	shirt, birthday
eɪ	date, table	aɪ	cry, eye
ɛ	bed, neck	aʊ	about, how
æ	bad, hand	ɔɪ	boy
ɑ	box, father	ɪr	here, near
ɔ	wash	ɛr	chair
oʊ	comb, post	ɑr	guitar, are
ʊ	book, good	ɔr	door, chore
u	boot, food, student	ʊr	tour
ʌ	but, mother		

Consonants

Symbol	Key Words	Symbol	Key Words
p	park, happy	t̬	butter, bottle
b	back, cabbage	tʔ	button
t	tie	ʃ	she, station, special, discussion
d	die	ʒ	leisure
k	came, kitchen, quarter	h	hot, who
g	game, go	m	men
tʃ	chicken, watch	n	sun, know
dʒ	jacket, orange	ŋ	sung, singer
f	face, photographer	w	week, white
v	vacation	l	light, long
θ	thing, math	r	rain, writer
ð	then, that	y	yes, use, music
s	city, psychology		
z	please, goes		

TOP NOTCH FUNDAMENTALS A
Vocabulary Booster

Vocabulary Booster

UNIT 1

🔊 **More occupations**

  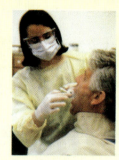 

1 an accountant   **2** a bank teller   **3** a dentist   **4** an electrician

5 a florist   **6** a gardener   **7** a grocery clerk

8 a hairdresser   **9** a mechanic   **10** a pharmacist   **11** a professor

12 a reporter   **13** a salesperson   **14** a travel agent

  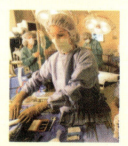 

15 a secretary   **16** a waiter   **17** a nurse   **18** a lawyer

On a separate sheet of paper, write five statements about the pictures. Use <u>He</u> or <u>She</u> and the verb <u>be</u>. For example: *He's an accountant.*

126 *Vocabulary Booster*

UNIT 2

More relationships

1 a supervisor
2 an employee

3 a teammate

More titles

1 Doctor [Smith] or Dr. [Smith]

2 Professor [Brown]

3 Captain [Jones]

On a separate sheet of paper, write three statements about the photos, using He's or She's and possessive adjectives. For example: *She's her supervisor.*

UNIT 3

More places in the neighborhood

1 a clothing store

2 an electronics store

3 a fire station

4 a police station

5 a shoe store

6 a toy store

7 a video store

8 a dry cleaners

9 a gas station

10 a hotel

11 a supermarket

12 a convenience store

13 a travel agency

14 a post office

15 a taxi stand

On a separate sheet of paper, write five questions about the places. For example:

Where's the clothing store?
Can I walk to the hotel?

Vocabulary Booster

UNIT 4

🔊 **More adjectives to describe people**

1 slim / thin

2 muscular

3 heavy

> On a separate sheet of paper, write a sentence for each photo. Use a form of <u>be</u> and the adverb <u>very</u> or <u>so</u>.
> For example: *He's very __.*

UNIT 5

🔊 **More events**

1 an exhibition

2 an opera

3 a football game

4 a volleyball game

5 a baseball game

6 a play

7 a speech

> On a separate sheet of paper, write five statements about the events. Use your own times and dates.
> For example: *There's an exhibition on Tuesday, June 15.*

128 **Vocabulary Booster**

TOP NOTCH FUNDAMENTALS A
Grammar Booster

Grammar Booster

The Grammar Booster is optional. It contains extra practice of each unit's grammar.

UNIT 1

1 Write each sentence again. Use a contraction.

1. He is an engineer. _He's an engineer._
2. We are teachers. _____
3. No, we are not. _____
4. They are not artists. _____
5. I am a student. _____
6. She is a chef. _____

2 Write the indefinite article <u>a</u> or <u>an</u> for each occupation.

1. _____ chef
2. _____ actor
3. _____ banker
4. _____ musician
5. _____ scientist
6. _____ architect
7. _____ photographer

3 Complete each sentence with the correct subject pronoun.

1. Mary is a student. _She_ is a student.
2. Ben is a student, too. _____ is a student, too.
3. My name is Nora. _____ am an artist.
4. Your occupation is doctor. _____ are a doctor.
5. Jane and Jason are scientists. _____ are scientists.

4 Write a question for each answer.

1. A: _Are you musicians_ ?
   B: Yes, we are. We're musicians.
2. A: _____ ?
   B: No, they're not teachers. They're scientists.
3. A: _____ ?
   B: Yes. Ann is a doctor.
4. A: _____ ?
   B: No. Ellen is a flight attendant. She's not a writer.
5. A: _____ ?
   B: Yes. I am a pilot.
6. A: _____ ?
   B: No. We're not flight attendants. We're pilots.

5 Write six proper nouns and six common nouns. Use capital and lowercase letters correctly.

Proper nouns

1. _____
2. _____
3. _____
4. _____
5. _____
6. _____

Common nouns

7. _____
8. _____
9. _____
10. _____
11. _____
12. _____

UNIT 2

1 **Write the correct possessive adjectives.**

1 Miss Kim is Mr. Smith's student. Mr. Smith is __her__ teacher.
2 Mr. Smith is Miss Kim's teacher. Miss Kim is _____ student.
3 Mrs. Krauss is John's teacher. Mrs. Krauss is _____ teacher.
4 John is Mrs. Krauss's student. John is _____ student.
5 Are _____ colleagues from Japan? No, they aren't. My colleagues are from Korea.
6 Mr. Bello is _____ teacher. I am _____ student.
7 Jake is not Mrs. Roy's student. He's _____ boss!
8 Mr. Gee is not Jim and Sue's teacher. He's _____ doctor.

2 **Complete the sentences about the people. Use He's from, She's from, or They're from.**

1 Ms. Tomiko Matsuda: _____ Hamamatsu, Japan.
2 Miss Berta Soliz: _____ Monterrey, Mexico.
3 Mr. and Mrs. Franz Heidelberg: _____ Berlin, Germany.
4 Mr. George Crandall: _____ Victoria, Canada.
5 Ms. Mary Mellon: _____ Melbourne, Australia.
6 Mr. Jake Hild and Ms. Betty Parker: _____ Los Angeles, US.
7 Mr. Cui Jing Wen: _____ Wuhan, China.
8 Ms. Noor Bahjat: _____ Cairo, Egypt.

3 **Complete the questions.**

1 _____ your name?
2 _____ are you from?
3 _____ his e-mail address?
4 _____ she a student?
5 _____ her phone number?
6 _____ they colleagues?
7 _____ he from China?
8 _____ their first names?

4 **Complete each question with the correct possessive adjective.**

1 A: What's _____ name?
   B: I'm Mrs. Barker.
2 A: What's _____ last name?
   B: My last name is Crandall.
3 A: What's _____ address?
   B: Mr. Marsh's address is 10 Main Street.
4 A: What's _____ e-mail address?
   B: Ms. Down's e-mail address? It's down5@unet.com.
5 A: What are _____ first names?
   B: They're Gary and Rita.
6 A: What's _____ phone number?
   B: Miss Gu's number is 555-0237.

Grammar Booster 137

UNIT 3

1 Write the sentences with contractions.

1. Where is the pharmacy? _Where's the pharmacy?_
2. It is down the street. _____
3. It is not on the right. _____
4. What is your name? _____
5. What is your e-mail address? _____
6. She is an architect. _____
7. I am a teacher. _____
8. You are my friend. _____
9. He is her neighbor. _____
10. They are my classmates. _____

2 Complete each sentence with an affirmative or a negative imperative.

1. _____ the bus to the restaurant. _____ walk.
2. _____ the bus to the bank.
3. _____ to the school. It's right over there, on the right.
4. _____ take a taxi to the bank. _____. It's across the street.

3 Complete the questions and answers. Use contractions when possible.

1. A: _____ the pharmacy?
   B: The pharmacy? _____ across the street.
2. A: _____ the newsstand?
   B: _____ down the street on the right.
3. A: _____ I _____ to the restaurant?
   B: No, don't walk there. _____ a taxi.
4. A: _____ do you go to school?
   B: Me? I go _____ motorcycle. _____ _____ you?

UNIT 4

1 Write questions. Use **Who's** or **Who are** and **he**, **she**, or **they**.

1. A: _Who's he_ _____?
   B: He's my grandfather.
2. A: _____?
   B: She's my mother.
3. A: _____?
   B: He's Mr. Ginn's grandson.
4. A: _____?
   B: They're Ms. Breslin's grandparents.
5. A: _____?
   B: She's Sam's wife.
6. A: _____?
   B: They're his wife and son.

Grammar Booster

2 Unscramble the words and write sentences. Use a form of <u>be</u>.

1 so / father / my / handsome <u>My father is so handsome.</u>
2 brother / very / her / short _____
3 grandchildren / cute / neighbor's / so / my _____
4 his / tall / not / sister / very _____
5 grandfather / very / old / my / not _____
6 friend / pretty / so / brother's / my _____

3 Complete the sentences. Use <u>have</u> or <u>has</u>.

1 I _____ two brothers.
2 She _____ one child.
3 They _____ four grandchildren.
4 We _____ six children.
5 You _____ ten brothers and sisters!
6 He _____ three sisters.

4 Complete the questions. Use <u>How old is</u> or <u>How old are</u>.

1 _____ your children?
2 _____ his son?
3 _____ her grandchildren?
4 _____ Nancy's sisters?
5 _____ Matt's daughter?
6 _____ their grandmother?

UNIT 5

1 Write a question for each answer. Use <u>What time</u>, <u>What day</u>, or <u>When</u>.

1 <u>What time is it?</u> It's six thirty.
2 _____ The party is at ten o'clock.
3 _____ The dinner is on Friday.
4 _____ The dance is at eleven thirty on Saturday.
5 _____ The concert is in May.
6 _____ The meeting is at noon.
7 _____ It's a quarter to two.
8 _____ The movie is on Wednesday.

2 Complete each sentence with <u>in</u>, <u>on</u>, or <u>at</u>.

1 The concert is _____ March.
2 The dinner is _____ Friday _____ 6:00.
3 The party is _____ April 4th _____ 9:00.
4 The movie is _____ 3:00 P.M. _____ Tuesday.
5 The game is _____ noon _____ Monday.
6 The meeting is _____ August 10th _____ 9:00 A.M.

Grammar Booster 139

UNIT 6

1 Complete each sentence with the correct form of the verb.

1 They _____ nice ties at this store.
   _{have}
2 She _____ a long, blue skirt for the party.
   _{want}
3 I _____ my shoes.
   _{like}
4 We _____ clean shirts.
   _{not have}
5 Our children _____ blue pants for school.
   _{not need}
6 _____ short skirts?
   _{she / like}
7 _____ new shoes?
   _{your wife / need}
8 _____ a suit for work?
   _{I / need}
9 Why _____ those old shoes?
   _{she / like}
10 Which shirt _____ for tomorrow?
   _{you / want}
11 _____ this sweater in extra large?
   _{they / have}

2 Answer each question.

1 What clothes do you need? _____
2 Do you need new shoes? _____
3 Why do you need new shoes? _____
4 Do you have a long skirt? _____
5 Do you like pink shirts? _____
6 Do you have a loose sweater? _____
7 Do you like expensive clothes? _____

UNIT 7

1 Write the third-person singular form of each verb.

1 shave _shaves_
2 brush _____
3 go _____
4 have _____
5 study _____
6 do _____
7 take _____
8 play _____
9 exercise _____
10 visit _____
11 practice _____
12 wash _____
13 come _____
14 change _____
15 make _____
16 get _____
17 comb _____
18 put _____
19 eat _____
20 watch _____
21 clean _____
22 read _____
23 check _____
24 listen _____

Grammar Booster

2 Complete each question with do or does

1 When _____ you go shopping?
2 What time _____ she make dinner?
3 How often _____ they clean the house?
4 What time _____ your son come home?
5 How often _____ your parents go out for dinner?
6 What time _____ you go to bed?
7 When _____ our teacher check e-mail?
8 How often _____ Alex do the laundry?

3 Unscramble the words and write sentences in the simple present tense.

1 usually / on weekends / go shopping / she *She usually goes shopping on weekends.*
2 go shopping / my sisters / on Fridays / sometimes _____
3 in the morning / never / check e-mail / I _____
4 always / my daughter/ to work / take the bus _____
5 we / to school / walk / never _____
6 sometimes / my brother / after work / visit his friends _____

4 Complete each response with do or does.

1 Who takes out the garbage in your house? My daughter _____.
2 Who washes the dishes in your family? I _____.
3 Who makes dinner? My parents _____.
4 Who does the laundry in your house? My brother _____.
5 Who watches TV before dinner? My granddaughter _____.
6 Who takes a bath in the evening? My sister _____.

Grammar Booster

Top Notch Pop Lyrics

What Do You Do? [Unit 1]
1:30

(CHORUS)
**What do you do?
What do you do?**

I'm a student.
You're a teacher.
She's a doctor.
He's a nurse.
What about you?
What do you do?
I'm a florist.
You're a gardener.
He's a waiter.
She's a chef.
Do-do-do-do…
That's what we do.
It's nice to meet you.
What's your name?
Can you spell that, please?
Thank you.
Yes, it's nice to meet you, too.

(CHORUS)

We are artists and musicians,
architects, and electricians.
How about you?
What do you do?
We are bankers,
we are dentists,
engineers, and flight attendants.
Do-do-do-do…
That's what we do.
Hi, I'm Linda. Are you John?
No, he's right over there.
Excuse me. Thank you very much.
Good-bye.
Do-do-do-do…
Do-do-do-do…
Do-do-do-do…
Do-do-do-do…

Excuse Me, Please [Unit 2]
1:46

(CHORUS)
**Excuse me—please excuse me.
What's your number?
What's your name?
I would love to get to know you,
and I hope you feel the same.**

I'll give you my e-mail address.
Write to me at my dot-com.
You can send a note in English
so I'll know
who it came from.
Excuse me—please excuse me.
Was that 0078?
Well, I think the class is starting,
and I don't
want to be late.

But it's really nice to meet you.
I'll be seeing you again.
Just call me on my cell phone
when you're looking for a friend.

(CHORUS)

So welcome to the classroom.
There's a seat right over there.
I'm sorry, but you're sitting in
our teacher's favorite chair!
Excuse me—please excuse me.
What's your number?
What's your name?

Tell Me All About It [Unit 4]
2:15

Tell me about your father.
He's a doctor and he's very tall.
And how about your mother?
She's a lawyer. That's her picture on
the wall.
Tell me about your brother.
He's an actor, and he's twenty-three.
And how about your sister?
She's an artist. Don't you think she looks
like me?

(CHORUS)
**Tell me about your family—
who they are and what they do.
Tell me all about it.
It's so nice to talk with you.**

Tell me about your family.
I have a brother and a sister, too.
And what about your parents?
Dad's a teacher, and my mother's eyes
are blue.

(CHORUS)

Who's the pretty girl in that photograph?
That one's me!
You look so cute!
Oh, that picture makes me laugh!
And who are the people there, right below
that one?
Let me see … that's my mom and dad.
They both look very young.

(CHORUS)

Tell me all about it.
Tell me all about it.

Let's Make a Date [Unit 5]
2:35

It's early in the evening—
6:15 P.M.
Here in New York City
a summer night begins.
I take the bus at seven
down the street from City Hall.
I walk around the corner
when I get your call.

(CHORUS)
**Let's make a date.
Let's celebrate.
Let's have a great time out.**

Let's meet in the Village
on Second Avenue
next to the museum there.
What time is good for you?
It's a quarter after seven.
There's a very good new show
weekdays at the theater.
Would you like to go?

(CHORUS)

Sounds great. What time's the show?
The first one is at eight.
And when's the second one?
The second show's too late.
OK, how do I get there?
The trains don't run at night.
No problem. Take a taxi.
The place is on the right.
Uh-oh! Are we late?
No, we're right on time.
It's 7:58.
Don't worry. We'll be fine!

(CHORUS)

On the Weekend [Unit 7]
3:15

(CHORUS)
**On the weekend,
when we go out,
there is always so much joy and laughter.
On the weekend,
we never think about
the days that come before and after.**

He gets up every morning.
Without warning, the bedside clock rings
the alarm.
So he gets dressed—
he does his best to be on time.
He combs his hair, goes down the stairs,
and makes some breakfast.
A bite to eat, and he feels fine.
Yes, he's on his way
to one more working day.

(CHORUS)

On Thursday night,
when he comes home from work,
he gets undressed, and if his room's a mess,
he cleans the house. Sometimes he takes
a rest.
Maybe he cooks something delicious,
and when he's done
he washes all the pots and dishes,
then goes to bed.
He knows the weekend's just ahead.

(CHORUS)

3:35

🔊 Home Is Where the Heart Is [Unit 8]

There's a house for everyone
with a garden in the sun.
There's a stairway to the stars.
Where is this house?
It isn't far.

(CHORUS)
Home is where the heart is.
Home is where the heart is.

She lives on the second floor.
There are flowers at her front door.
There's a window with a breeze.
Love and kindness are the keys.

(CHORUS)

There's a room with a view of the sea.
Would you like to go there with me?

(CHORUS)

4:17

🔊 Fruit Salad, Baby [Unit 10]

You never eat eggs for breakfast.
You don't drink coffee or tea.
I always end up cooking for you
when you're here with me.
I want to make something delicious,
'cause I like you a lot.
I'm checking my refrigerator,
and this is what I've got:

(CHORUS)
How about a fruit salad, baby—
apples, oranges, bananas too?
Well, here you go now, honey.
Good food coming up for me and you.

Are there any cans or bottles
or boxes on the shelf?
I put my dishes on the counter.
I mix everything well.

(CHORUS)

Chop and drain it.
Slice and dice it.
Mix and serve
with an ounce of love.
Pass your glass.
What are you drinking?
Tell me what dish
I am thinking of?

(CHORUS)

4:34

🔊 My Favorite Day [Unit 11]

Last night we walked together.
It seems so long ago.
And we just talked and talked.
Where did the time go?
We saw the moonlit ocean
across the sandy beach.
The waves of summer fell,
barely out of reach.

(CHORUS)
Yes, that was then,
and this is now,
and all I do is think about
yesterday,
my favorite day of the week.

When I woke up this morning,
my feelings were so strong.
I put my pen to paper,
and I wrote this song.
I'm glad I got to know you.
You really made me smile.
My heart belonged to you
for a little while.

(CHORUS)

It was wonderful to be with you.
We had so much to say.
It was awful when we waved good-bye.
Why did it end that way?

(CHORUS)

5:16

🔊 She Can't Play Guitar [Unit 13]

She can paint a pretty picture.
She can draw well every day.
She can dance and she can sing,
but she can't play guitar.
She can sew a dress so nicely,
and she does it beautifully.
She can knit a hundred sweaters,
but she can't play guitar.

(CHORUS)
And now it's too late.
She thinks it's too hard.
Her happy smile fades,
'cause she can't play guitar.

She can drive around the city.
She can fix a broken car.
She can be a great mechanic,
but she can't play guitar.

(CHORUS)
And she says,
"Could you please help me?
When did you learn?
Was it hard? Not at all?
Are my hands too small?"
She can cook a meal so nicely
in the kitchen, and there are
lots of things that she does well,
but she can't play guitar.

(CHORUS)

5:33

🔊 I Wasn't Born Yesterday [Unit 14]

I went to school and learned the lessons
of the human heart.
I got an education in
psychology and art.
It doesn't matter what you say.
I know the silly games you play.

(CHORUS)
I wasn't born yesterday.
I wasn't born yesterday.

Well, pretty soon I graduated
with a good degree.
It took some time to understand
the way you treated me,
and it's too great a price to pay.
I've had enough, and anyway,

(CHORUS)

So you think I'd like to marry you
and be your pretty wife?
Well, that's too bad, I'm sorry, now.
Grow up and get a life!
It doesn't matter what you say.
I know the silly games you play.

(CHORUS)

SECOND EDITION

TOP NOTCH
FUNDAMENTALS A

Workbook

Joan Saslow • Allen Ascher

With Julie C. Rouse

UNIT 1: Names and Occupations

LESSON 1

1. Match the occupations with the pictures. Write the letter on the line.

1. _____ a teacher
2. _____ an artist
3. _____ an athlete
4. _____ a musician
5. _____ a flight attendant
6. _____ a banker
7. _____ a singer

a.
b.
c.
d.
e.
f.
g.

2. FAMOUS PEOPLE. What are their occupations? Write sentences. Use contractions.

1. Frank Gehry: _He's an architect_____.
2. Lance Armstrong: _____.
3. Matt Damon: _____.

3 Complete the conversation between Hee-Young Lim and Constantina Tomescu.

Hee-Young Lim: Hi. I'm Hee-Young.

Constantina Tomescu: Hi, _____.

Hee-Young Lim: Nice to meet you, Constantina.

Constantina Tomescu: _____.

Hee-Young Lim: What do you do?

Constantina Tomescu: _____.
_____?

Hee-Young Lim: I'm a musician.

LESSON 2

4 Match the occupations that go together. Write the letter on the line.

1. _c_ a singer
2. ____ a teacher
3. ____ an architect
4. ____ a pilot

a. a student
b. a flight attendant
c. a musician
d. an engineer

5 Circle the occupation that is different.

1. scientist   engineer   chef   doctor
2. singer   manager   actor   athlete
3. banker   artist   musician photographer

6 Look at the people going to work. Write sentences about their occupations. Use contractions.

1. _She's an artist_ _____.
2. _____.
3. _____.
4. _____.
5. _____.
6. _____.

W2 UNIT 1

7 Complete the sentences with names.

1. My favorite singer is _____.
2. My favorite actor is _____.
3. My favorite athlete is _____.
4. _____ is a famous artist.
5. _____ is a famous musician.
6. _____ is a famous writer.

8 Read the list. Then look at the pictures and complete the conversations.

Name	Occupation
Anna Madden	Pilot
Maggie Gill	Singer
Julia Santos	Doctor
Grace Lund	Scientist
Emily Parson	Student
Caroline Benson	Banker
Nicole Locke	Student

Are you Maggie?

1. No, I'm not. I'm Grace.

Are you Anna?

2. _____

Are you Caroline?

3. _____

Are you Emily and Nicole?

4. _____

9 Read about Madonna.

Tom is a famous singer. He's also an actor. And he's a writer, too. Three occupations! The name of his first children's book is *The English Roses*. Tom is the writer, but he's not the artist. The artist is Jeffrey Fulvimari. *The English Roses* is now a collection of twelve books.

Now answer the questions. Check ✓ the boxes.

1. What are Tom's occupations?
   ☐ artist   ☐ photographer   ☐ teacher
   ☐ actor   ☐ singer   ☐ writer

2. What is Jeffrey Fulvimari's occupation?
   ☐ writer   ☐ actor   ☐ artist

10 Circle the occupation that is not spelled correctly.

1. engineer	doctor	arkitect	athlete
2. shef	banker	teacher	singer
3. scientist	fotographer	musician	manager
4. writer	pilot	actor	flite attendant

Now write the words correctly.

5. _____
6. _____
7. _____
8. _____

W4   UNIT 1

LESSON 3

11 Rewrite the sentences. Capitalize the proper nouns.

1. john landry is a chef in paris.
   _____.

2. isabel hunter is from canada. She's an architect.
   _____.

3. alex quinn is a pilot. He's in tokyo today.
   _____.

12 Write proper and common nouns. Capitalize the proper nouns.

1. Your name: _____
2. Your occupation: _____
3. Your teacher's name: _____
4. Matt Damon's occupation: _____

13 Read the occupations in the box. Count the syllables. Write each occupation in the correct place on the chart.

| athlete | chef | ~~engineer~~ | actor | manager |
| musician | photographer | scientist | singer | writer |

1 syllable	2 syllables	3 syllables	4 syllables
		engineer	

14 Choose the correct response. Circle the letter.

1. How are you?
   a. I'm Samantha.   b. Great.   c. Take care.
2. What do you do?
   a. I'm a manager.   b. Fine, thanks.   c. I'm Jim.
3. Are you Lucy?
   a. Yes, she is.   b. OK. See you!   c. No, I'm not.
4. How do you spell that?
   a. Right over there.   b. T-O-M-E-S-C-U.   c. I'm a writer. And you?

JUST FOR FUN

1 A RIDDLE FOR YOU!

Ms. Adams, Ms. Banks, Ms. Clark, and Ms. Dare have four different occupations—**engineer, architect, doctor,** and **scientist** (but NOT in that order).

Read the statements.

Ms. Adams and Ms. Clark are not doctors.

Ms. Banks and Ms. Clark are not scientists.

Ms. Clark and Ms. Dare are not architects.

Ms. Adams is not a scientist.

Now write an occupation for each person.

Ms. Adams: _____

Ms. Banks: _____

Ms. Clark: _____

Ms. Dare: _____

Source: Adapted from norfolkacademy.org.

2 WORD FIND. Look across (→) and down (↓). Circle the eight occupations. Then write the occupations on the lines.

```
N E I M E P A E N N B K R P P E
M O E T E O A M E S U I H A T L
A E L P O L L H N C N N N T R Y
N T W E S A A S A I H H R R L I
A O R H T E T T R E T E T E N C
G K I E N P H E S N A H N E S A
E N T P C R L A M T R E N S R E
R T E A E A E I N I N N E R N U
K A R A S H T A A S E R E R A T
O A T N Y T E I U T E H G R N M
E C P H O T O G R A P H E R H E
R T N A S M B E N G I N E E R B
N O E N R A E E E E R A E R E L
A R O K P E G N E R A N U U H E
O T T B A N K E R T L E G C T E
N N K R N N E R N R T B I G E T
```

Source: Created with spellbuilder.com.

Riddle: Ms. Adams: architect; Ms. Banks: doctor; Ms. Clark: engineer; Ms. Dare: scientist

UNIT 2 About People

LESSON 1

1 Look at the pictures. Write possessive adjectives.

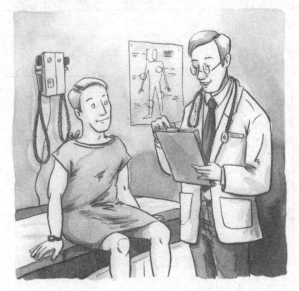

1. _His_ doctor is Dr. Brown.

2. _____ teacher is Ms. Jalbert.

3. _____ boss is Mr. Lin.

4. _____ neighbors are Mr. and Mrs. Rivers.

2 Look at the pictures. Complete the sentences about relationships. Use possessive nouns.

1. He is _Eric's classmate_____.
2. She is _____.

3. They are _____.
4. He is _____.

3 Complete the sentences.

1. Audrey is _____ classmate.
   _{I / my}
2. We're _____ students.
   _{Mr. Haber's / Mr. Haber}
3. Who is _____ manager?
   _{you / your}
4. Ms. Miller and Mr. Sullivan are _____ colleagues.
   _{our / we}
5. Are _____ your neighbors?
   _{they / their}
6. Dr. Franklin isn't _____ doctor.
   _{Bill / Bill's}

4 Match the description and the relationship. Write the letter on the line.

1. ____ Caleb and I are managers. Our company is Infotech. Our boss is Mr. Jackson.
2. ____ Anna's address is 32 Arbor Street. Zoe's address is 34 Arbor Street.
3. ____ Ryan and Josh are students in the same class. Ms. Foster is their teacher.
4. ____ Jessica and I are classmates. She's my neighbor, too.

a. They're classmates.
b. We're colleagues.
c. They're neighbors.
d. We're friends.

5 Look at Joe's list and Amy's list for their party.

JOE'S LIST
Kristin – friend
Jeff – friend
Robert and Julie – friends
Mark – classmate
Gary and Ann – neighbors

Amy's List
Samantha – colleague
Peter – colleague
Katherine – boss
Gary and Ann – neighbors
Robert and Julie – friends

Now write sentences about the people. Use possessive adjectives.

1. Peter: Peter is her colleague.
2. Mark: _____.
3. Gary and Ann: _____.
4. Katherine: _____.
5. Kristin: _____.

6 YOUR RELATIONSHIPS. Complete the chart with names.

Classmates or Colleagues	Neighbors	Friends

7 Choose a friend and a classmate from Exercise 6. Introduce them. Complete the conversation.

1. **You:** _____, this is _____.
   _____'s my classmate.
2. **Your friend:** Hi, _____.
3. **Your classmate:** Hi, _____. Nice to meet you.
   Your friend: Nice to meet you, too.
   Your classmate: What do you do?
4. **Your friend:** I'm _____. And you?
5. **Your classmate:** I'm _____.
   Your friend: Where are you from?
6. **Your classmate:** I'm from _____.

LESSON 2

8 Fill out the form for a friend, a neighbor, or a colleague.

☐ Mr.
☐ Mrs. _____ _____
☐ Miss   *first name*   *last name*
☐ Ms.

Now complete the conversation between the person and a clerk.

1. **Clerk:** Hi. What's your last name, please?

   _____ : _____.

2. **Clerk:** And your first name?

   _____ : My first name? _____.

3. **Clerk:** How do you spell that?

   _____ : _____.

4. **Clerk:** Thank you.

   _____ : _____.

9 Complete the sentences. Use real names and relationships.

1. Mr. _____ is my _____.
2. Mr. and Mrs. _____ are my _____.
3. Ms. _____ is my _____.
4. Miss _____ is my _____.

LESSON 3

10 Complete the address book with information for three friends.

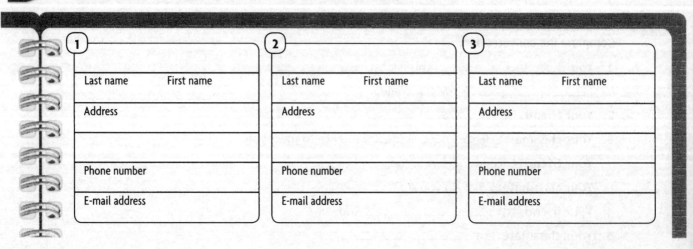

11 Write the answers in words.

1. eleven + six = _____
2. nineteen − twelve = _____
3. three × five = _____
4. twenty ÷ two = _____

12 Look at the business cards. Read the responses. Then write questions with <u>What's</u>. Use possessive nouns or possessive adjectives.

1. A: <u>What's Ms. Harrison's first name</u>? B: Kate.
2. A: <u>What's her address</u>? B: 77 York St.
3. A: _____? B: jeff.silver@edi.com
4. A: _____? B: He's a manager.
5. A: _____? B: 0208 755 8050.
6. A: _____? B: 28 Manor Street.

13 Answer the questions. Use your own information.

1. What's your first name? _____
2. What's your last name? _____
3. What's your occupation? _____
4. What's your address? _____
5. What's your phone number? _____
6. What's your e-mail address? _____

JUST FOR FUN

1 TAKE A GUESS! Write the next number in words.

1. three, six, nine, twelve, fifteen, _____
2. one, two, four, eight, _____
3. twenty, one, nineteen, two, eighteen, three, _____

Source: From riddlenut.com.

2 Complete the puzzle.

Across

4. We are _____. Our addresses are 15 and 17 Pine Street.
5. The Musee du Louvre's _____ is 99 Rue de Rivoli, Paris.
9. Frank Gehry's occupation
10. Her name is Linda Reid. Reid is her _____ name.

Down

1. Mr. Bryant is Andy's teacher. Andy is _____ student.
2. Their address is 11 Palm Street, and their _____ is (661) 555-4485.
3. Banana Yoshimoto's title
6. Allison's _____ address is allie@mail.net.
7. Flight attendants and pilots are _____.
8. A=one, B=two, C=three, . . . N= _____

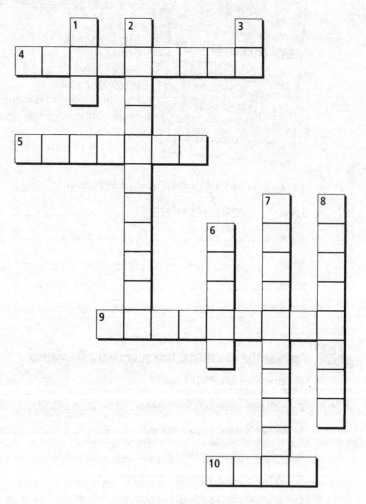

Source: Created with Discovery's Puzzlemaker.

Guess: 1. eighteen; 2. sixteen; 3. seventeen

W12 UNIT 2

UNIT 3 Places and How to Get There

LESSON 1

1 Write the names of places in your neighborhood.

1. a restaurant: _____
2. a bank: _____
3. a bookstore: _____
4. a pharmacy: _____
5. a school: _____

2 Read the directions. Label the places on the map.

- The school is across the street.
- The bookstore is around the corner.
- The bank is next to the bookstore.
- The newsstand is down the street on the left.
- The pharmacy is down the street on the right.

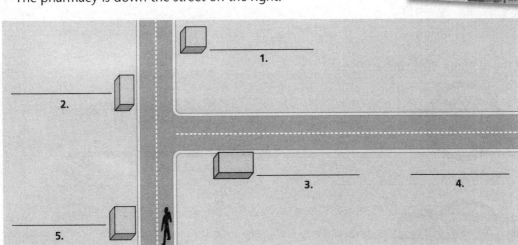

3 Read the answers. Then complete the questions with <u>Where's</u> or <u>What's</u>.

1. A: _____ the address?   B: 214 New Street.
2. A: _____ the bookstore?   B: It's down the street on the left.
3. A: _____ the pharmacy?   B: It's across the street.
4. A: _____ Lisa's occupation?   B: She's a photographer.
5. A: _____ his e-mail address? B: Rob123@mail.net.
6. A: _____ your friend's restaurant? B: It's around the corner.

W13

4 Look at the pictures. Write questions and answers. Follow the model.

1.
2.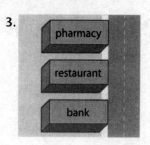
3.
4.

1. A: _Where's the school_ ? B: _It's around the corner_ .
2. A: _____ ? B: _____ .
3. A: _____ ? B: _____ .
4. A: _____ ? B: _____ .

LESSON 2

5 Complete the conversation. Tell a friend how to get to your school.

1. Your friend: Can I walk to the school?
   YOU: _____

2. Your friend: OK. And where is it?
   YOU: _____

3. Your friend: OK. Thanks!
   YOU: _____

6 Look at the pictures. Write imperatives.

1. _Don't drive_ .

2. _____ .

3. _____ .

4. _____ .

5. _____ .

7 Tell a new classmate how to go places from school. Use an affirmative and a negative imperative.

Example: to a bookstore: _Take the bus. Don't walk._

1. to a bookstore: _____
2. to a bank: _____
3. to a pharmacy: _____
4. to a restaurant: _____

8 Look at the pictures. Write a sentence with an imperative and a sentence about the location. Follow the model.

1.    _Take a taxi to the bookstore_.
   It's next to the bank.

2.    _____.
   _____.

3.    _____.
   _____.

4. _____.
   _____.

Places and How to Get There W15

9 Look at the pictures. Write questions. Follow the model.

1. Can I walk to the bookstore ?

2. _____ ?

3. _____ ?

4. _____ ?

LESSON 3

10 Look at the pictures. Answer the questions. Use a <u>by</u> phrase.

1. How does she go home?
   By subway.

2. How does he go to the bookstore?
   _____.

3. How do they go to work?
   _____.

4. How does she go to school?
   _____.

11 How do you go places? Read the sentences. Write <u>T</u> for sentences that are true for you and <u>F</u> for sentences that are false for you.

1. ____ I go to school by bicycle.
2. ____ I take a taxi to restaurants.
3. ____ I go to work by train.
4. ____ I go home from school by bus.
5. ____ I walk to the bookstore.
6. ____ I go to work by moped.
7. ____ I take the subway to the bank.

JUST FOR FUN

1 **A RIDDLE FOR YOU!** Read the clues. Then write the places on the lines.

- The bookstore is between the restaurant and the pharmacy.
- The bank is not next to the bookstore.
- The restaurant is next to the bank.
- The pharmacy is not on the left.

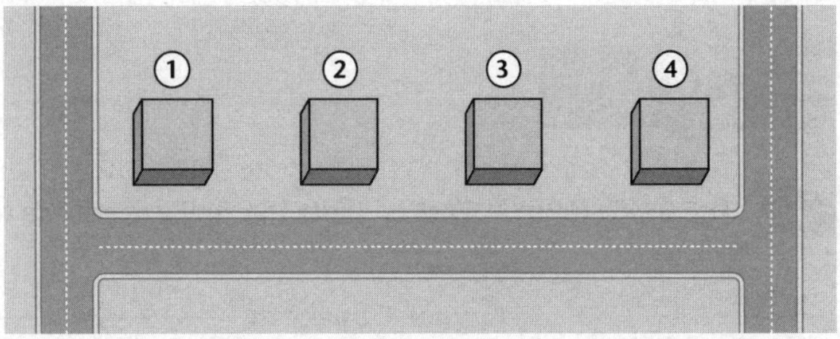

1. _____
2. _____
3. _____
4. _____

2 **WORD FIND.** Look across (→) and down (↓). Circle the eight means of transportation. Then write the means of transportation on the lines.

_____
_____
_____
_____
_____
_____
_____
_____

```
C U S O G Z Z S H Z Z F B M H
H S H P R F A I A L J S I B I
E U P H S I R Y T O X X S W S
K B A N M O T O R C Y C L E C
G W A B O W M T A J W F F F X
U A C N P Z P L I Q I Y M F Y
T Y N C E S P I N B O Y G T H
Z M Y K D C I A S O A K B N T
R W E N M B W M N H T F I X E
T I Y T L Q Q E P O R U C P Q
Z A I U U R T S T A X I Y S W
E G A K K L R H K B U S C H S
X K U K M U N C A R G T L H Z
M J F N J R Q W G V F B E X Y
S C X T A U E O B Q W S V B P
```

Source: Created with tools.atozteacherstuff.com

Riddle: 1. bank; 2. restaurant; 3. bookstore; 4. pharmacy

Places and How to Get There W17

UNIT 4 Family

LESSON 1

1 THE BRITISH ROYAL FAMILY. Write the family member's relationship to Queen Elizabeth on the line.

Queen Elizabeth — Prince Philip
1. _her husband_

Prince Charles
2. _____

Princess Anne
3. _____

Prince Andrew

Prince Edward

Prince William | Prince Harry
4. _____

Peter Phillips | Zara Phillips

Princess Beatrice | Princess Eugenie
5. _____

Lady Louise Windsor

2 Look at Queen Elizabeth's family again. Complete the sentences.

1. Prince Harry is Prince William's _____.
2. Princess Anne is Zara Phillips's _____.
3. Queen Elizabeth and Prince Philip are Prince Charles's _____.
4. Prince Philip is Prince Harry's _____.
5. Queen Elizabeth is Prince Philip's _____.
6. Prince William and Prince Harry are Prince Charles's _____.
7. Prince Andrew is Princess Eugenie's _____.
8. Queen Elizabeth is Peter Phillips's _____.
9. Princess Eugenie is Princess Beatrice's _____.
10. William, Harry, Peter, Zara, Beatrice, Eugenie, and Louise are Queen Elizabeth's _____.

3 Complete the conversation. Write <u>What</u>, <u>Where</u>, or <u>Who</u>.

1. Andrew: _____'s that?
   Hannah: That's my brother.
2. Andrew: _____'s your brother's first name?
   Hannah: Paul.
3. Andrew: _____'s your sister?
   Hannah: She's right there, on the left.
4. Andrew: _____'s that?
   Hannah: My grandmother.
5. Andrew: _____ her last name?
   Hannah: Connor.
6. Andrew: _____ are your parents?
   Hannah: They're here, next to my grandmother.

4 Read the answers. Then write questions with <u>Who</u>.

1. A: _____?
   B: They're my brothers.
2. A: _____?
   B: That's my husband.
3. A: _____?
   B: He's my father.
4. A: _____?
   B: They're my grandparents.
5. A: _____?
   B: She's my sister.

5 Answer the questions.

1. Who are you? _____.
2. Who's your teacher? _____.
3. Who are your classmates? (Name three.) _____.

LESSON 2

6 Write the names of three relatives, friends, neighbors, or classmates. Then complete the chart.

Name	Relationship	Age	Occupation	pretty	handsome	cute	short	tall	old	young
Michelle	sister	26	manager	✓				✓		✓

Family

7. Unscramble the words. Write sentences.

1. brother / tall / is / My / very _____.
2. handsome, / He / too / very / is _____.
3. your / Are / pretty / sisters _____?
4. is / daughter / young / Her _____.
5. cute / so / is / She _____!

8. Describe your relatives. Write sentences.

_____
_____
_____
_____
_____
_____
_____
_____

LESSON 3

9. Look at the photos and read.

Hi, I'm Kate. There are five people in my family. I have two sisters. Their names are Megan and Jane. Jane and I are students. Megan is a doctor.

Hello. My name is Edgar. My wife's name is Anna. I'm an engineer, and she's an architect. We have two children. Riley is our son, and Reese is our daughter.

Hello. I'm George. My wife Carol and I are grandparents. We have three children and two grandchildren. Our granddaughter is Sophia. Our grandson is Jake.

Now answer the questions.

1. Who's Jake? _He's George's grandson_____.
2. Who's Anna? _____.
3. Who's Jane? _____.
4. Who are Riley and Reese? _____.
5. Who are George and Carol? _____.
6. Who's a doctor? _____.

10 Look at the picture. Write sentences with <u>have</u> or <u>has</u>.

1. Julia: <u>She has two brothers   </u>.
2. Rose: _____.
3. Barbara and Martin: _____.
4. Dan and Michael: _____.
5. Louis: _____.

11 Write the next number in words.

1. twenty-one, twenty-eight, thirty-five, forty-two, _____
2. four, eight, sixteen, _____, sixty-four
3. ninety-nine, _____, seventy-five, sixty-three, fifty-one
4. ten, eleven, twenty-one, thirty-two, fifty-three, _____

12 Complete each sentence with <u>have</u> or <u>has</u>. Then choose the correct response. Circle the letter.

1. Matthew _____ two sisters.
   a. How old is she?   b. How old are they?
2. Mark and Jamie _____ a daughter.
   a. How old is he?   b. How old is she?
3. I _____ a brother and a sister.
   a. How old is your brother?   b. How old is my sister?
4. We _____ a son.
   a. What's your name?   b. What's his name?

Family W21

JUST FOR FUN

1 **A RIDDLE FOR YOU!** Read the sentence. Then answer the question.

Brothers and sisters have I none, but that man's father is my father's son.
Who is "that man"? _____

Source: From thinks.com.

2 Complete the puzzle.

Across

3. Julie's grandmother is ninety-five. She's _____.
6. Sons and daughters
7. A good-looking woman is _____.
8. Not tall
10. Her grandchildren are very _____. They're one and three years old.
11. A good-looking man is _____.

Down

1. The English alphabet has _____ letters.
2. My father's mother is my _____.
4. Abigail Breslin's occupation
5. His daughter's son is his _____.
7. Mother and father
9. Joan Lin is Jackie Chan's _____.

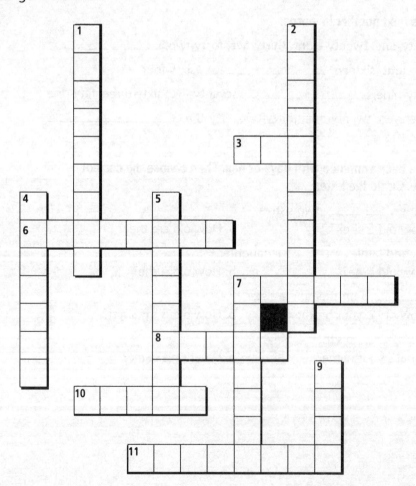

Source: Created with Discovery's Puzzlemaker.

Riddle: My son

UNIT 5
Events and Times

LESSON 1

1 Match the times.

1. __c__ It's half past ten.   a. 6:45
2. _____ It's four o'clock.   b. 8:55
3. _____ It's noon.   c. 10:30
4. _____ It's a quarter after two.   d. 12:00 P.M.
5. _____ It's five to nine.   e. 4:00
6. _____ It's six ten.   f. 6:10
7. _____ It's a quarter to seven.   g. 12:00 A.M.
8. _____ It's midnight.   h. 2:15

2 Look at the pictures. Are the people <u>early</u>, <u>late</u>, or <u>on time</u>? Write sentences.

1. _____.   2. _____.   3. _____.

W23

3 Look at the pictures. Then complete the conversation.

LESSON 2

4 Write an occupation for each event.

1. a concert: _a singer_
2. a movie: _____
3. a game: _____
4. a dinner: _____

5 When is your English class? Circle the day or days. Write the times.

Monday	Tuesday	Wednesday	Thursday	Friday	Saturday	Sunday

6 What events are in your city or town this week? Complete the chart.

Name	Event	Day	Time	Place
Hee-Young Lim	Concert	Saturday	7:00 p.m.	Music Center

W24   UNIT 5

7 Look at the posters.

Now check true or false.

	true	false
1. The game is on Sunday.	☐	☐
2. The movie is at 7:10 on Wednesday.	☐	☐
3. The dinner is at half past seven.	☐	☐
4. The concert is at three o'clock.	☐	☐
5. The movie is at 3:40 on Saturday.	☐	☐

8 Look at the posters in Exercise 7 again. Complete the questions and answers.

1. A: _____? B: It's _____ one o'clock.
2. A: _____? B: It's _____ Friday _____ a quarter to eight.
3. A: _____? B: It's _____ Thursday.
4. A: _____? B: It's _____ Sunday _____ 3:00.

9 Complete the conversation. Use the times and days on the posters in Exercise 7.

1. **You:** Hi, _____. How are you?

    Your friend: Fine, thanks. And you?

2. **You:** _____. Look. There's a _____ on _____.

    Your friend: Great! What time?

3. **You:** _____.

    Your friend: OK. Let's meet at _____.

Events and Times **W25**

LESSON 3

10 Match the ordinal numbers with the people. Draw lines.

fifth   first   ninth   eleventh   seventh   thirteenth

second   twelfth   sixth   eighth   fourth   fifteenth

11 Look at the pictures. Write the months for each type of weather where you live.

1. _____
2. _____
3. _____

12 Complete the sentences with an ordinal number or a month.

1. October is the _____ month of the year.
2. _____ is the fifth month of the year.
3. _____ is the second month of the year.
4. March is the _____ month of the year.
5. December is the _____ month of the year.
6. _____ is the eleventh month of the year.
7. June is the _____ month of the year.
8. _____ is the eighth month of the year.

13 Complete the conversations. Use the prepositions in, on, and at.

1. A: When's your birthday? B: It's _____ March. It's _____ March 11th.
2. A: Am I late? B: No, you're _____ time.
3. A: What time is the party? B: It's _____ 1:30.
4. A: Is the game at 9:15 tonight? B: No, it's _____ the afternoon, _____ 3:45.
5. A: When's the play? B: _____ Saturday, _____ 8:00.
6. A: What time's the movie? B: It's _____ midnight.
7. A: Is the dinner in January? B: Yes, it's _____ the 19th.
8. A: There's a concert at 10:00. B: _____ night or _____ the morning?

14 Look at the invitation.

Now answer the questions. Write complete sentences.
1. What month is the party? _It's in March._
2. What date is the party? _____
3. What day is the party? _____
4. What time's the party? _____
5. Where's the restaurant? _____

JUST FOR FUN

1 Fill in the answers. Then look at the numbers under the lines. Write the letters in the puzzle.

1. A dinner, or a concert

   $\underline{}\,\underline{}\,\underline{}\,\underline{}\,\underline{}\,\underline{}\,\underline{}$
     12   3 10   1

2. The class is on weekdays—Mondays, Wednesdays, and _____.

   $\underline{}\,\underline{}\,\underline{}\,\underline{}\,\underline{}\,\underline{}\,\underline{}$
    8 4 5   11 6

3. An event with athletes

   $\underline{}\,\underline{}\,\underline{}\,\underline{}\,\underline{}$
       13   7

4. April is the _____ month of the year.

   $\underline{}\,\underline{}\,\underline{}\,\underline{}\,\underline{}\,\underline{}$
    9   2

Puzzle

" $\underline{}\,\underline{}\,\underline{}\,\underline{}\,\underline{}\ \underline{}\,\underline{}\ \underline{}\,\underline{}\,\underline{}\ \underline{}\,\underline{}\,\underline{}\ \underline{}\,\underline{}\,\underline{}\,\underline{}\,\underline{}\,\underline{}\,\underline{}\,\underline{}$."
  1 2 3 4 3   5 6   1 5 7 3   8 9 4   3 10 3 4 11 1 2 5 12 13

—Thomas Edison, inventor (U.S.)

2 Complete the puzzle.

Across

5. This month has twenty-eight days.
7. Jana's birthday is March 12th. What's her sign?
9. The movie's at 10:15. It's a quarter to ten now. You're _____.
10. Good _____! (at 7:00 P.M.)
13. Good _____! (at 7:00 A.M.)

Down

1. The ninth month of the year
2. The fourth weekday
3. The first day of the weekend
4. The time in New Delhi when it's noon in New York
6. Q is the _____ letter in the alphabet.
8. The baseball _____ is on Friday.
11. 12:00 A.M.
12. 12:00 P.M.

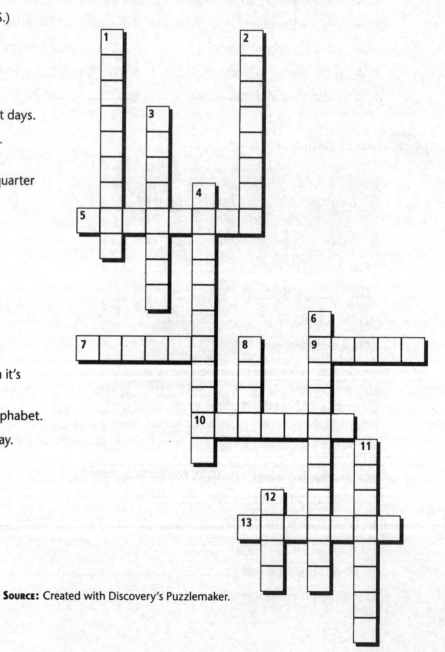

SOURCE: Created with Discovery's Puzzlemaker.

UNIT 6 Clothes

LESSON 1

1 Write the names of the clothes.

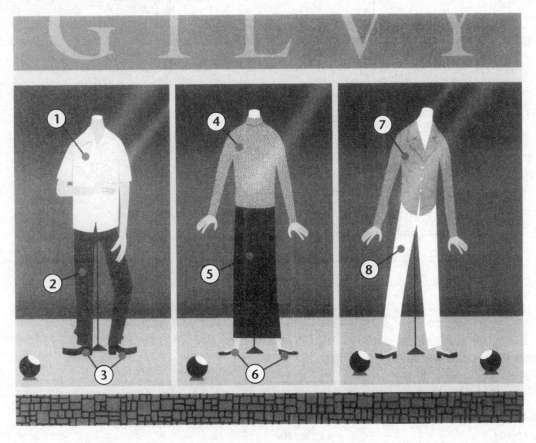

1. _____
2. _____
3. _____
4. _____
5. _____
6. _____
7. _____
8. _____

2 Circle one of the clothing items in each picture. Write a sentence with **I like** and <u>this</u>, <u>that</u>, <u>these</u> or <u>those</u>.

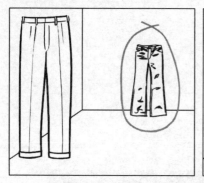 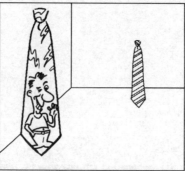 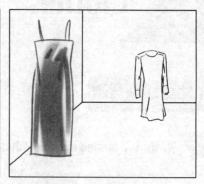

Example: _I like those pants_ 1. _____ 2. _____

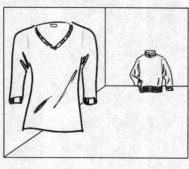 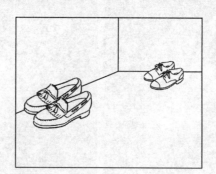

3. _____ 4. _____

3 Write sentences. Use words from each list.

| I / My sister / brother / My parents / My classmates / My neighbor / My friends / My friend and I / My teacher | + | like / likes | + | restaurants / bookstores / weekends / motorcycles / parties / dances / movies / concerts |

1. _My friends like parties_.
2. _____.
3. _____.
4. _____.
5. _____.

4 Look at the pictures. Complete the sentences. Use <u>want</u>, <u>need</u>, or <u>have</u>.

1. __They have__ a daughter.

2. _____ a jacket.

3. _____ that car.

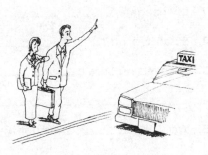

4. _____ a taxi.

5. _____ a moped.

6. _____ that tie.

5 Look at the pictures. Compliment each person on his or her clothes.

①  ②

1. _____
   _____
   _____

2. _____
   _____
   _____

Clothes **W31**

LESSON 2

6 Complete the sentences about yourself. Use <u>like</u> or <u>don't like</u>.

Example: ___I don't like___ red jackets.

1. _____ brown suits.
2. _____ purple pants.
3. _____ black sweaters.
4. _____ white shoes.
5. _____ blue shirts / blouses.

7 Complete the sentences. Write the simple present tense of the verb.

1. My daughters _____ those dresses.
   _{want}
2. Susan's friend _____ her skirt.
   _{not like}
3. Michael and Steven _____ suits.
   _{not have}
4. _____ you _____ a jacket?
   _{have}
5. We _____ shoes for the party.
   _{need}
6. _____ Anthony _____ this tie?
   _{want}
7. _____ Ryan _____ large or extra large?
   _{need}
8. They _____ this blouse in white.
   _{not have}

8 Look at the clothes. Write a question. Ask for the color or size in parentheses. Then complete the short answer.

①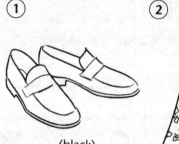
(black)

②
(small)

③
(brown)

④
(large)

1. ___Do you have these shoes in black___? No, ___we don't___.
2. _____? Yes, _____.
3. _____? Yes, _____.
4. _____? No, _____.

W32   UNIT 6

LESSON 3

9 Write sentences about yourself. Use have / don't have, want / don't want, or need / don't need.

Example: expensive shoes: _I don't need expensive shoes_.

1. a gray suit: _____.
2. new pants: _____.
3. a red sweater: _____.
4. a white shirt / blouse: _____.
5. a long jacket: _____.

10 Read about Elena and Marina.

> Elena and Marina are looking for new clothes. They're at Fashionistas, a new clothes store. They need clothes for work. Elena is a manager, and Marina is a musician. Elena's suit is old, and she needs a new one. She wants new shoes, too. Marina needs a black dress for a concert on Saturday.
>
> Fashionistas has a black suit, a gray suit, a brown suit, and a red suit in Elena's size. She likes the gray suit. Fashionistas has a short dress and a long dress in black. Marina wants the short dress. The long dress is very expensive. Fashionistas doesn't have shoes. Elena says, "Look! There's a shoe store across the street."

Now read the answers. Then write questions. Use Why, What, or Which.

1. A: _____? B: Because her suit is old.
2. A: _____? B: A suit and shoes.
3. A: _____? B: A black dress.
4. A: _____? B: The gray suit.
5. A: _____? B: The short dress.

11 Plan your clothes for next week. Write on the calendar.

Monday	Tuesday	Wednesday	Thursday	Friday	Saturday	Sunday
gray pants black sweater new black shoes						

12 Look at the pictures. Complete the questions and the answers.

"What do you think of _these pants_?"

"What do you think of _____?"

1. YOU _____
   _____.

2. YOU _____
   _____.

"What do you think of _____?"

"What do you think of _____?"

3. YOU _____
   _____.

4. YOU _____
   _____.

JUST FOR FUN

1. TAKE A GUESS! Match the numbers with the letters to make these colors.

1. _____ green
2. _____ orange
3. _____ purple
4. _____ brown
5. _____ gray

a. red and green
b. yellow and blue
c. yellow and red
d. black and white
e. blue and red

2. WORD FIND. Look across (→) and down (↓). Circle the ten clothes and the ten colors. Then write the clothes and colors on the lines.

```
I P U I K E K T S I R E I B Y C
J T S S S E K B R O W N R E L R
A U K W L W T T G U R B L E I D
C K I E L H E E U U R E G P G O
K W R A E I G R E L E A R A R K
E T T T K T C T T R A R E L A A
T I U E E E W O O A B L U E Y L
H E I R Y E L L O W N Y I D E H
G G R E E N R R N Y E L S R D O
T R E D P N K E S E O S S B R R
B G R E U E K I E E R H U R E U
L A S G R N O B A R A I I I S W
A U H A P I G S L R N R T L S T
C W O L L P A N T S G T B O I S
K R E O E K E A H A E B U T R Y
N H L R R H H R I B L O U S E E
```

SOURCE: Created with spellbuilders.com.

Clothes

_____ _____
_____ _____
_____ _____
_____ _____
_____ _____

Colors

_____ _____
_____ _____
_____ _____
_____ _____
_____ _____

Guess: 1. b; 2. c; 3. e; 4. a; 5. d

Clothes W35

UNIT 7 Activities

LESSON 1

1 YOUR MORNING ACTIVITIES. Put the activities in order. Write ordinal numbers (1st, 2nd, . . .) on the lines. Write an **X** next to the activities you don't do.

_____ take a shower / bath

_____ eat breakfast

_____ get up

_____ shave

_____ get dressed

_____ brush my teeth

_____ comb / brush my hair

Choose your first three morning activities. What time do you do them?

Example: _I get up at 7:00_____.

1. _____.
2. _____.
3. _____.

2 Look at the activities and the times. Write sentences in the simple present tense.

1. _She comes home at 6:30_____.

2. _____.

3. _____.

4. _____.

3 Write the name of a family member or friend. Check his or her activities.

Name: _____

☐ takes a shower in the evening   ☐ studies after dinner
☐ takes a shower in the morning   ☐ watches TV after dinner
☐ doesn't eat breakfast   ☐ gets up early on weekends
☐ eats a large breakfast   ☐ gets up late on the weekend

Now write sentences about this person.

4 Look at the responses. Write questions with <u>When</u> or <u>What time</u>.

1. A: *When does Karina take a shower* _____?
   B: Karina takes a shower in the morning.

2. A: _____?
   B: Robert goes to bed after midnight. He's an evening person.

3. A: _____?
   B: My children? They watch TV on weekends, in the morning.

4. A: _____?
   B: I study after dinner.

5. A: _____?
   B: Julia gets up at 5:00 A.M. on weekdays.

6. A: _____?
   B: They come home early—before 5:00 P.M.

5 Complete the conversation.

Are you a morning person or an evening person?

1. YOU _____.

And why do you say that?

2. YOU _____.

LESSON 2

6 On a typical weekday, do you . . . ? Check always, usually, sometimes, or never.

	always	usually	sometimes	never
1. eat breakfast	☐	☐	☐	☐
2. watch TV in the evening	☐	☐	☐	☐
3. take a shower at night	☐	☐	☐	☐
4. read after 10:00 P.M.	☐	☐	☐	☐
5. exercise in the morning	☐	☐	☐	☐
6. take a nap in the afternoon	☐	☐	☐	☐
7. go out for lunch	☐	☐	☐	☐

On a typical weekend, do you . . . ? Check always, usually, sometimes, or never.

	always	usually	sometimes	never
1. visit friends	☐	☐	☐	☐
2. study	☐	☐	☐	☐
3. go to the movies	☐	☐	☐	☐
4. play soccer	☐	☐	☐	☐
5. check e-mail	☐	☐	☐	☐
6. go out for dinner	☐	☐	☐	☐

7 Look at your answers in Exercise 6. Write five sentences about your activities. Follow the model.

Example: _On weekdays, I usually exercise in the morning_.

1. _____.
2. _____.
3. _____.
4. _____.
5. _____.

8 Think about the leisure activities of family members and friends. Complete the chart.

Name / Relationship	Activity	Time expression	Frequency
grandfather	take a nap	in the afternoon	usually

Now write sentences about the leisure activities of family members and friends. Use your chart.

Example: _My grandfather usually takes a nap in the afternoon_____.

1. _____.
2. _____.
3. _____.
4. _____.
5. _____.

LESSON 3

9 Look at Larry's weekly schedule.

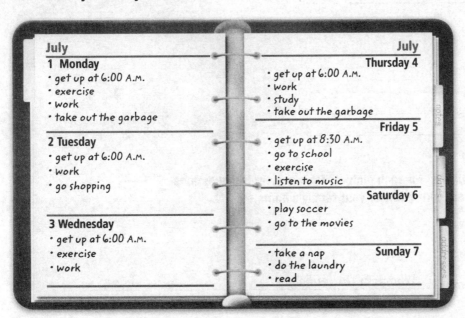

Now write questions with <u>How often</u> and complete the answers.

1. A: _How often does Larry go to school_____?
   B: He _____ once a week.

2. A: _____?
   B: He _____ twice a week.

3. A: _____?
   B: He _____ three times a week.

4. A: _____?
   B: He _____ four times a week.

10 Look at Larry's schedule in exercise 9 again. Answer the questions.

1. When does Larry work? _____.
2. When does he go to school? _____.
3. What's his typical day like? _____.
4. What time does he get up on Fridays? _____.
5. What does he do in his free time? _____.

11 Look at the pictures. Then write sentences about the household chores Mr. and Mrs. Rand do.

Mr. Rand
1. _____.
2. _____.

Mrs. Rand
3. _____.
4. _____.
5. _____.

12 Write a question with <u>Who</u> for each picture. Then answer the questions with information about your home or your family's home.

Example: __Who does the laundry__? __I do__.

1. _____? _____.
2. _____? _____.
3. _____? _____.
4. _____? _____.

W40   UNIT 7

JUST FOR FUN

1 A RIDDLE FOR YOU!

What comes once in an afternoon, twice in a week, but never in a day or month?

(Hint: It comes once in the alphabet.)

Answer: _____

2 WORD FIND. Look across (→) and down (↓). Circle the fourteen activities. Then write the activities in the correct column.

```
W A T C H T V U C E A K A U H I T
E P N A C O H C L H S O I K V R I
K L W A S H T H E D I S H E S E A
G A L M S G A N A M C T M N M A M
E Y L M G O A L N K B A O H A D K
T S O R O D T N T S D K W W K W O
V O A G T A A T H A A E T N E V O
A C E D O N S C E U N A H I D A I
C C S A W C Y H H O M B E A I W I
U E N U O I C S O E U A L O N H E
U R S R R N B T U T E T A D N S E
M L N S K G E G S O O H W A E A E
C H C B D O T H E L A U N D R Y D
T E L I S T E N T O M U S I C H D
T E T A K E A N A P E N H A O I E
L H T I A K N T T U E W W N S S A
```

SOURCE: Created with ed.helper.com.

Chores / Work activities

_____

_____

_____

_____

_____

_____

_____

Leisure activities

_____

_____

_____

_____

_____

_____

_____

Riddle: the letter e

Activities **W41**

UNITS 1-7 Review

1 Circle the word or phrase that is different.

1. (athlete)	classmate	neighbor	colleague
2. doctor	engineer	(pharmacy)	scientist
3. last name	(weekend)	address	phone number
4. subway	moped	train	(game)
5. (brother)	daughter	wife	grandmother
6. tall	(new)	handsome	young
7. concert	party	restaurant	(movie)
8. skirt	blouse	dress	(tie)
9. listen to music	(do the laundry)	visit friends	go to the movies
10. get up	shave	come home	(eat breakfast)

2 Read the ad for an event.

Women's Soccer
Russia and Brazil

The Sports Center
Saturday, May 15th
1:00 P.M.

Tickets on sale now!
www.sportstix.com

Now write a question for each answer.

1. **A:** _____?
   B: A soccer game.

2. **A:** _____?
   B: The Sports Center.

3. **A:** _____?
   B: At one o'clock.

4. **A:** _____?
   B: On Saturday, May 15th.

3 Read about Salma Hayek.

> This is Salma Hayek. She's an actor. She's from Mexico, but her name is Arabic. Her father's family is from Lebanon. Her mother is Mexican. Her father is a businessman, and her mother is an opera singer. She has one brother, Sami Hayek. Salma Hayek's birthday is September 2, 1966. She's a Virgo. She is short and very pretty. In September 2007, Hayek became a mother. She and her husband have a daughter. Her name is Valentina Paloma.
>
> Salma Hayek's 2002 movie *Frida* is not very old, but it's already a classic. It is the winner of two Academy Awards—for music and for makeup. The movie is about the famous Mexican artist Frida Kahlo. Hayek is Frida in the movie. Alfred Molina is her husband, the artist Diego Rivera. Many of Hayek's friends are in the movie. The acting is great. The colors, art, clothes, and music in *Frida* are beautiful.

Source: Adapted from www.imdb.com

Now answer the questions.

1. What does Salma Hayek do? *She's an actor*
2. Is she from Lebanon? *No she isn't. She's from Mexico.*
3. Does Hayek have brothers and sisters? *She has 1 brother*
4. When is her birthday? *September 2, 1966*
5. How old is she? *52*
6. Is she tall? *yes, yes, she does is*
7. How old is her daughter? *It doesn't say.*
8. What is her daughter's first name? *Valentina Paloma*

4 Compare Frida Kahlo and Salma Hayek. Complete the chart. Use the reading in Exercise 3.

	Frida Kahlo	Salma Hayek
Occupation	artist	
Nationality	from Mexico	
Nationality of father	from Germany	
Nationality of mother	from Mexico	
Brothers and sisters	3 sisters, no brothers	
Birthday	July 6, 1907	

5 Choose one family member, friend, neighbor, or colleague. Complete the information.

1. Name: _____
2. Relationship to you: _____
3. Occupation: _____
4. Birthday, age (how old?), sign: _____
5. Adjectives to describe the person: _____
6. Leisure activities: _____

Now write about this person. Use the information above.

_____
_____
_____
_____
_____
_____
_____

OPTIONAL VOCABULARY BOOSTER ACTIVITIES

1 Look at the pictures. Write a yes / no question with be and a short answer. Use the words in parentheses.

1.
A: _Is he a bank teller_ ?
   (bank teller)
B: _No, he's not_ .

2.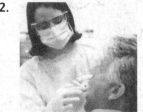
A: _____ ?
   (doctor)
B: _____ .

3.
A: _____ ?
   (lawyer)
B: _____ .

4.
A: _____ ?
   (electrician)
B: _____ .

5.
A: _____ ?
   (florist)
B: _____ .

2 Look at the pictures. Write answers to the questions. Remember to capitalize proper nouns.

Sam

Ms. Smith

Alex

Ellen Lane

Peter Jansson

1. What is the grocery clerk's name? _His name is Sam_ .
2. What is the pharmacist's name? _____ .
3. What is the waiter's name? _____ .
4. What is the travel agent's first name? _____ .
5. What is the professor's last name? _____ .

3 Answer a friend's questions about your neighborhood.

1. How do you go to the supermarket? _____
2. Can I walk to the dry cleaners? _____
3. Where's the video store? _____

4 Which events do you like? Number the events from 1 to 8 in the order you like them.

____ plays   ____ art exhibitions
____ operas   ____ baseball games
____ speeches   ____ volleyball games
                          ____ football games

Review **W45**

5 Write this, that, these, or those and the names of the clothes.

Do you like _____ 1. ?

I need _____ 2. , but I want _____ 3. .

Are _____ 4. black or blue?

Look at _____ 5. . They're really nice.

6 Look at the pictures. Ask for a different color or size. Write yes / no questions with have.

1. Do you have these sandals in red _____ ?

2. _____ ?

3. _____?

4. _____?

5. _____?

7 Look at the pictures and the answers. Write the questions.

1. **A:** _How often do dust_ ? you

   B: Twice a month.

2. **A:** _____ you _____?

   B: On Sundays.

3. **A:** _____?

   B: My wife does.

4. **A:** _____?

   B: Yes, I do.

About the Authors

Joan Saslow

Joan Saslow has taught in a variety of programs in South America and the United States. She is author of a number of multi-level integrated-skills courses for adults and young adults: *Ready to Go: Language, Lifeskills, and Civics; Workplace Plus: Living and Working in English;* and of *Literacy Plus.* She is also author of *English in Context: Reading Comprehension for Science and Technology.* Ms. Saslow was the series director of *True Colors* and *True Voices.* She participates in the English Language Specialist Program in the U.S. Department of State's Bureau of Educational and Cultural Affairs.

Allen Ascher

Allen Ascher has been a teacher and a teacher trainer in China and the United States and taught in the TESOL Certificate Program at the New School in New York. He was also academic director of the International English Language Institute at Hunter College. Mr. Ascher is author of the "Teaching Speaking" module of *Teacher Development Interactive,* an online multimedia teacher-training program, and of *Think about Editing: A Grammar Editing Guide for ESL.*

Both Ms. Saslow and Mr. Ascher are frequent and popular speakers at professional conferences and international gatherings of EFL and ESL teachers.

Authors' Acknowledgments

The authors are indebted to these reviewers who provided extensive and detailed feedback and suggestions for the second edition of *Top Notch* as well as the hundreds of teachers who participated in surveys and focus groups.

Manuel Aguilar Díaz, El Cultural Trujillo, Peru • **Manal Al Jordi,** Expression Training Company, Kuwait • **José Luis Ames Portacarrero,** El Cultural Arequipa, Peru • **Vanessa de Andrade,** CCBEU Inter Americano, Curitiba, Brazil • **Rossana Aragón Castro,** ICPNA Cusco, Peru • **Jennifer Ballesteros,** Universidad del Valle de México, Campus Tlalpan, Mexico City, Mexico • **Brad Bawtinheimer,** PROULEX, Guadalajara, Mexico • **Carolina Bermeo,** Universidad Central, Bogotá, Colombia • **Zulma Buitrago,** Universidad Pedagógica Nacional, Bogotá, Colombia • **Fabiola R. Cabello,** Idiomas Católica, Lima, Peru • **Emma Campo Collante,** Universidad Central Bogotá, Colombia • **Viviane de Cássia Santos Carlini,** Spectrum Line, Pouso Alegre, Brazil • **Fanny Castelo,** ICPNA Cusco, Peru • **José Luis Castro Moreno,** Universidad de León, Mexico • **Mei Chia-Hong,** Southern Taiwan University (STUT), Taiwan • **Guven Ciftci,** Faith University, Turkey • **Freddy Correa Montenegro,** Centro Colombo Americano, Cali, Colombia • **Alicia Craman de Carmand,** Idiomas Católica, Lima, Peru • **Jesús G. Díaz Osío,** Florida National College, Miami, USA • **Ruth Domínguez,** Universidad Central Bogotá, Colombia • **Roxana Echave,** El Cultural Arequipa, Peru • **Angélica Escobar Chávez,** Universidad de León, Mexico • **John Fieldeldy,** College of Engineering, Nihon University, Aizuwakamatsu-shi, Japan • **Herlinda Flores,** Centro de Idiomas Universidad Veracruzana, Mexico • **Claudia Franco,** Universidad Pedagógica Nacional, Colombia • **Andrea Fredricks,** Embassy CES, San Francisco, USA • **Chen-Chen Fu,** National Kaoshiung First Science Technology University, Taiwan • **María Irma Gallegos Peláez,** Universidad del Valle de México, Mexico City, Mexico • **Carolina García Carbajal,** El Cultural Arequipa, Peru • **Claudia Gavancho Terrazas,** ICPNA Cusco, Peru • **Adriana Gómez,** Centro Colombo Americano, Bogotá, Colombia • **Raphaël Goossens,** ICPNA Cusco, Peru • **Carlo Granados,** Universidad Central, Bogotá, Colombia • **Ralph Grayson,** Idiomas Católica, Lima, Peru • **Murat Gultekin,** Faith University, Turkey • **Monika Hennessey,** ICPNA Chiclayo, Peru • **Lidia Hernández Medina,** Universidad del Valle de México, Mexico City, Mexico • **Jesse Huang,** National Central University, Taiwan • **Eric Charles Jones,** Seoul University of Technology, South Korea • **Jun-Chen Kuo,** Tajen University, Taiwan • **Susan Krieger,** Embassy CES, San Francisco, USA • **Robert Labelle,** Centre for Training and Development, Dawson College, Canada • **Erin Lemaistre,** Chung-Ang University, South Korea • **Eleanor S. Leu,** Soochow University, Taiwan • **Yihui Li (Stella Li),** Fooyin University, Taiwan • **Chin-Fan Lin,** Shih Hsin University, Taiwan • **Linda Lin,** Tatung Institute of Technology, Taiwan • **Kristen Lindblom,** Embassy CES, San Francisco, USA • **Ricardo López,** PROULEX, Guadalajara, Mexico • **Neil Macleod,** Kansai Gaidai University, Osaka, Japan • **Robyn McMurray,** Pusan National University, South Korea • **Paula Medina,** London Language Institute, Canada • **María Teresa Meléndez de Elorreaga,** ICPNA Chiclayo, Peru • **Sandra Cecilia Mora Espejo,** Universidad del Valle de México, Campus Tlalpan, Mexico City, Mexico • **Ricardo Nausa,** Centro Colombo Americano, Bogotá, Colombia • **Tim Newfields,** Tokyo University Faculty of Economics, Tokyo, Japan • **Mónica Nomberto,** ICPNA Chiclayo, Peru • **Scarlett Ostojic,** Idiomas Católica, Lima, Peru • **Ana Cristina Ochoa,** CCBEU Inter Americano, Curitiba, Brazil • **Doralba Pérez,** Universidad Pedagógica Nacional, Bogotá, Colombia • **David Perez Montalvo,** ICPNA Cusco, Peru • **Wahrena Elizabeth Pfeister,** University of Suwon, South Korea • **Wayne Allen Pfeister,** University of Suwon, South Korea • **Cecilia Ponce de León,** ICPNA Cusco, Peru • **Andrea Rebonato,** CCBEU Inter Americano, Curitiba, Brazil • **Elizabeth Rodríguez López,** El Cultural Trujillo, Peru • **Olga Rodríguez Romero,** El Cultural Trujillo, Peru • **Timothy Samuelson,** BridgeEnglish, Denver, USA • **Enrique Sánchez Guzmán,** PROULEX, Guadalajara, Mexico • **Letícia Santos,** ICBEU Ibiá, Brazil • **Lyndsay Shaeffer,** Embassy CES, San Francisco, USA • **John Eric Sherman,** Hong Ik University, South Korea • **João Vitor Soares,** NACC, São Paulo, Brazil • **Elena Sudakova,** English Language Center, Kiev, Ukraine • **Richard Swingle,** Kansai Gaidai College, Osaka, Japan • **Sandrine Ting,** St. John's University, Taiwan • **Shu-Ping Tsai,** Fooyin University, Taiwan • **José Luis Urbina Hurtado,** Universidad de León, Mexico • **Monica Urteaga,** Idiomas Católica, Lima, Peru • **Juan Carlos Villafuerte,** ICPNA Cusco, Peru • **Dr. Wen-hsien Yang,** National Kaohsiung Hospitality College, Kaohsiung, Taiwan • **Holger Zamora,** ICPNA Cusco, Peru.